TAROT

UNVEILED

AN OCCULTIST'S PERSPECTIVE
ON THE CARDS

AUTHOR BIOGRAPHY

Gordon Strong (1948–2023) was a writer, speaker, and workshop host. He was well-known in the UK and the West Coast of America. He has published several books on myths, magic, and sacred monuments and numerous novels. Music, laughter with friends, and walking were his other pursuits.

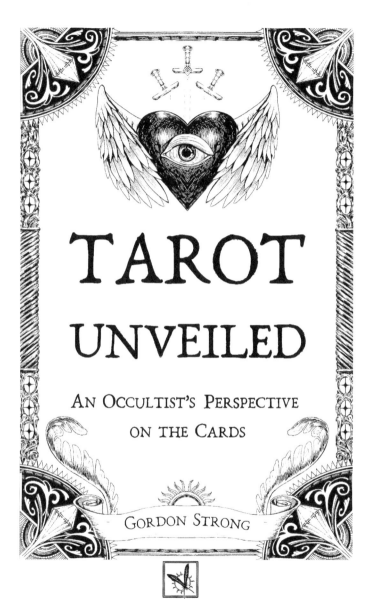

TAROT
UNVEILED

An Occultist's Perspective
on the Cards

GORDON STRONG

Chicago, IL

Paperback ISBN: 978-1-959883-72-2
Library of Congress Control Number on file.

Published by:
Crossed Crow Books, LLC
6934 N Glenwood Ave, Suite C
Chicago, IL 60626
www.crossedcrowbooks.com

Printed in the United States of America.

IBI

IN MEMORIAM

**Gordon Selby Strong
(1948-2023)
Bristol, UK**

*In my writing I'm always upholding the traditional
virtues of nobility and respect and, above all, love.*

—Gordon Selby Strong

CONTENTS

"*The most ancient manner of writing was that of representing things by persons, and by words, by which was understood something altogether different from what was expressed. In such a manner, indeed, that nothing was literally true just as it was written, but under these narratives something allegorical was understood.*"

—Emmanuel Swedenborg

INTRODUCTION

The game of chess was once considered to be a distillation of all philosophy. The tarot has come to be regarded as having the same qualities: the cards are a microcosm, a universe in miniature that serves as a distillation of wisdom and magick. The tarot is divided into two sections: the Major and the Minor Arcana. The former, as we shall see, deals with the great questions of human existence and thus, the great mysteries as well. Let us not underestimate the term *mystery*. I have studied the cards for the greater part of my life and yet the tarot continues to withhold some of its secrets from me. No reader's knowledge of the cards can ever equal the magick of the cards themselves, and that is how it should be. The tarot is part of the *magickal imagination* and renews its enchantment constantly. By doing this, it maintains its power and the continual fascination it exercises over humanity. Magick is not something that only certain individuals are capable of; it is all around us and within us, for everything is a metaphor of experience. It is beyond time, beyond class or culture—beyond humankind, even.

The student of magick knows that the tarot is a series of illustrations of magickal philosophy. It is a tower of strength (and sometimes a Falling Tower) in an unsettled world. The common or consensus of reality, what might be termed the *mass consciousness,* is very different from the *universal mind*—a manifestation of the divine will which exists beyond ordinary consciousness. Separate from the material world (the superficial appearance of things), the universal mind is the force that determines what actually occurs on the material plane. Things in our world change almost arbitrarily—triumph turns to disaster, gain to loss. Why? Many cannot figure it out and conclude that life is meaningless. They may turn to religion in the hope of obtaining answers (and just as quickly reject them), but their souls are rarely at peace.

What modern humanity cannot perceive is the ebb and flow of existence—the divine rhythm. There is a distinction between "consciousness" and "perception." The former applies to a state of experiencing existence, the latter to the mechanics of a particular phenomenon within that experience. How do we "perceive" anything? Understanding the mechanics of perception has always been a problem for cognitive science. The more we learn about how we understand and interact with the world, the less becomes clear. How does the brain sort, codify, and draw meaning from the information it receives from the senses? Not only that, but perception also includes the ability to recognize, detect, and understand. Modern humanity fears any change in their situation which they cannot predict. It is not surprising that their efforts to control the world are so much of the time in vain. They will not acknowledge, as their ancestors did, the power of nature to manifest all things in due season. By working with the unconscious forces that surround us, what magicians refer to as the "inner planes," a greater knowledge of the universe is gained. A balanced view of the world is particularly essential now, for we exist in a time when hallucination and falsity have almost become a way of life. If we are prepared to make the journey into the inner world, all starts to become clear. Even the knowledge that these forces exist suddenly gives a freshness and strength to our lives. The shadows that were once threatening fall away and any fear of the unknown disappears. Illusions still glitter, but there is no chance they will turn to gold.

In grouping various tarot cards under a theme, I have tried to show how the cards form a comprehensive whole. Be patient; let the tarot take you into its confidence at its own pace. *Understanding* is the key here, as well as the acquiring of information. I always feel that I am on good terms with the citizenry of the tarot world. On their behalf, I bid you welcome.

CHAPTER ONE

*"The tarot could be described as God's Picture Book,
or it could be likened to a game of chess...."*

—Lady Frieda Harris

A Brief History[1]

In the fourteenth century, a pack of fifty-two cards was used for gaming in many Islamic countries. They bore the symbols of Cups, Coins, Swords, and Staves. It is this pack that became our ordinary "playing cards." These, the Minor Arcana, combined with the twenty-two "trumps" (The Major Arcana) and the addition of four "pages" comprise the modern *tarot*. The origin of the word is in no way clear. In 1778, Antoine Court de Gébelin spoke of *Tarraux*, a game of Egyptian origin. He speculated that the name may be composed of the two words *Tar* and *Rha* or *Rho*, meaning "Royal Road." Other suggestions are that the name derives from the Sanskrit *Taru*, meaning "deck of cards," and *Torah*, the Hebraic Law. The first card decks bearing the name of tarot originated during the Renaissance in Milan, Italy. Renaissance decks sometimes bore the names of nearby rivers, so it may also be of significance that a river called Taro flows not far from Milan.

The Egyptian *Book of Thoth* has a direct link with the tarot, but it is certainly not the only source of its panoply of images. The archetypes that are depicted in the Major Arcana come from many different cultures. A number of images that served as illustrations for the Renaissance poet

---

1   A detailed history of the tarot would take up most of this book. It is a fascinating, confusing, and inconclusive tale, but one well worth investigating for the student, if only for the historical as well as the esoteric element.

Petrarch's book *The Triumphs* have found their way into the tarot, which has also given us the word "Trumps" to describe the cards of the Major Arcana (Triumphs is *Trionfos* in the original Italian). The Emperor is Teutonic, The Hierophant has origins in the Russian Orthodox Church, and The Wheel of Fortune stems from India, while Death probably refers to the medieval plagues.

We are now used to a deck containing seventy-eight cards, but this was not always so, as Bill Butler tells us: "An Italian game, Tarrocchino, incorporating one hundred cards came to be devised in the next century. Included in it were all the signs of the Zodiac, the Virtues, in short all that was necessary for the proper instruction of the young."[2]

The tarot as we know it today makes its first appearance in several decks created during the fifteenth century in the court of Filippo Maria Visconti in Milan. While many Renaissance rulers patronized artists, Filippo Maria Visconti collected and patronized esoteric scholars. While some of Visconti's decks, notably the Cary-Yale Tarot, include more cards than the present deck (it had princes and princesses), it is the deck known as the Visconti-Sforza Tarot that most closely matches the present deck, with the exception of the Fool, who is represented by a card called The Wild Man.[3] Painted by the artist Bonifacio Bembo (b. 1420–d. after 1477), this deck—though incomplete—is regarded as a

---

2   Butler, Bill, *The Definitive Tarot* (Hutchinson, 1975) p. 3.

3   This character was quite common in medieval folklore and still exists today. Some have seen him romping through the streets of the city of Basel in Switzerland during the February folk festival known as *Fasnacht*. His costume still bears a strong resemblance to the Wild Man of the Visconti-Sforza deck.

masterpiece of Renaissance art and has been often recreated in contemporary times.[4] Reproductions of the Visconti-Sforza and Cary-Yale decks can be easily purchased in metaphysical bookstores and online.

In 1760, the Marseilles pack of Nicholas Conver was engraved and printed. It is only in the late nineteenth century that a tradition linking astrology and the Kabbalah emerged,[5] although A.E. Waite,[6] who systematized the pack that bears his name, deliberately avoided giving precedence to the Kabbalah as the basis for the symbolism within.[7] The Marseilles Tarot was the most familiar deck until the images of the Rider-Waite pack. Arthur Edward Waite, the foremost scholar among the members of the Hermetic Order of the Golden Dawn, initiated the plan to develop a tarot deck inspired by the teachings of the Golden Dawn. As his partner in the project, he chose Pamela Colman Smith, artist and bohemian, who had joined the Golden Dawn in 1901 and who was known as "Pixie" because of her small size, childlike appearance, and effervescent personality.

---

4   More specifically, the deck painted by Bembo is incomplete because six of the cards vary somewhat in style from Bembo's major works and may have been substituted later to replace lost cards.

5   *Qabala* is the spelling based upon actual Hebrew letters, whereas *Kabbalah* is a Westernized spelling.

6   The pack continues to be referred to as the Rider-Waite, though that name is now trademarked by U.S. Games, which published its version of Smith and Waite's deck in 1971. Rider was simply the original publisher, though, and it is heartening to see that Pamela Colman Smith is now receiving the acclaim she deserves and being recognized not only as a gifted artist but a visionary as well.

7   Robert Wang is particularly succinct on this point: "Some, especially Jewish scholars, have been quite hostile toward an attachment of Qabalistic ideas to the tarot...." In: Robert Wang, *The Qabalistic Tarot, A Textbook of Mystical Philosophy* (Marcus Aurelius Press, 2004).

Waite brought her his ideas for the cards of the Major Arcana. He was an outstanding scholar but couldn't draw, so he wrote his ideas down in the form of letters to Smith and left the imagery to her. When the Sola Busco Tarot, created in Italy in the late fifteenth century, was on exhibition at the British Museum, Waite and Smith went to see it. The Major Arcana of the Sola Busco is somewhat anomalous and doesn't match the standard images, but it was the Minor Arcana which proved to be truly unique. Until then, the Minor Arcana had no specific images, only pictures of the objects for which the suit was named. The Sola Busco was unusual because some of the Minor Arcana cards included images.

Waite and Smith's visit to the British Museum proved to be of enormous significance for the history of the Western esoteric tradition, for it gave Waite and Smith the idea to use pictorial images for the Minor Arcana cards. There is no question that Smith was directly influenced by the Sola Busco Tarot; her Three of Swords is a precise match with the earlier Renaissance deck. Waite had almost nothing to do with the images on the fifty-six cards of the Minor Arcana—all of them appear to have been created solely by Pamela Colman Smith. Hers was the first deck to include images for all of the Minor Arcana cards, and it took her only six months to complete all seventy-eight cards.

The so-called Rider-Waite deck (or more accurately the Smith-Waite deck) was published in London by William Rider and Sons in 1909. It has often been noted that the women associated with the Golden Dawn, for example Florence Farr and Moira Mathers, have been under-represented in the literature about the Order. A study of the development of the Waite-Smith Tarot—of which only a brief summary has been given here—clearly reveals Pamela Colman Smith as the principal creative force behind the world's most popular tarot deck. It is only now that she is beginning to achieve the recognition she so richly deserves.[8] The imagery in this deck is what we will be referencing throughout this book.

Divination

The tarot gives us insights into another world, the sphere that exists alongside the conscious world. The "real" world is only a collection of ciphers that reflect the rhythms of the inner planes. We can never *control* these rhythms as they are not at our command, but we may interpret and pass on our observations of them. Bill Butler is characteristically forthright:

> *The cards are not magic. They do not tell the future, they cannot evaluate the past…. As shadows by their nature are not 'fixed' it seems likely that shadows of the future are no more fixed. What is reflected is possibility…. The tarot can be conceived as a window overlooking any point in time…like the I Ching, [it] can be used as a map….[9]*

---

8   A version of the deck titled the *Centennial Smith-Waite* was released in 2009 to commemorate the one-hundredth anniversary of the initial deck's creation. This version embraced the original colour palette chosen by Pamela Coleman Smith herself.

9   Butler, Bill, *The Definitive Tarot* (Hutchinson, 1975).

Those of us who have made the tarot part of our inner world know its wondrous and enchanting power. Yet, readers should never force the tarot upon anyone! If any individual does not wish to share in its munificence, then that is their prerogative.

I have written at some length regarding the reading of cards and having one's cards read, and so I shall make only a few observations here.[10] It is worth remembering that, in the practice of magick, psychism is seen only as a means to an end. For this reason, some mystical schools regard divination as an irrelevance, maintaining that the search for enlightenment should be the only goal. In my view, the quest for enlightenment serves only to reinforce the respect that the tarot deserves. The student should beware of assuming that they can master the tarot quickly. It is an instrument of such complexity that it can never be mastered, for it always has new things to teach. The way that the student approaches the tarot determines if it will reveal those secrets.

Intuitive readers who get astonishing results certainly exist, but they are few. My own approach is to be both scholarly and intuitive. As a teacher of the tarot, I need to be able to make its ways comprehensible to my students. I delight in the discussions we have in our workshops, but I doubt that I can actually *teach* a student to be a tarot reader. Sometimes I encounter students that I think will make excellent readers because they have a natural ability, but again, this is rare. The path of experience and growing insight is the one that most of us have had to take, and it will serve you down the long road.

---

10   In Strong, Gordon, *Question of Magick* (Flash Magic Press, 2007).

I would not seek to deter anyone who aspires to be a tarot reader from pursuing such a goal. Equally, I would make it plain to anyone who intends to read professionally that they must be absolutely certain of what they are doing. Even more important is why they are doing it—motive is all. I make the same strictures with regard to those who would practice magick. These are deep waters, and being out of one's depth in the mystical tides can be extremely alarming indeed. That said—let us be encouraging! Assuming that our novice reader is set upon their path, let us consider what experiences they are likely to encounter.

As with any skill, reading improves with practice. The first attempts at a coherent picture from the cards will be accompanied by uncertainty and hesitation, but this will soon disappear. Keep it simple; most problems have a beginning, a middle, and an outcome. The reader who is a beginner tends to talk too much: make a habit of pausing between delivering your insights and allow the querent to take in and fully comprehend what you are saying. A light touch and a little humour go a long way to diffusing any tension in the atmosphere. Remember, the situation may be difficult or strange for your clients and it is your responsibility to make them feel at ease.

Equally, the reader should be relaxed and flexible in his approach. Never be too rigid in any interpretation, nor should you let personal prejudice affect your insights.[11] We are all

---

11   This is the weakness of instructional guides to the tarot. Interesting they may be and often helpful, but if they are simply followed to the letter, your readings will lack any real insight.

capable of making mistakes, so let us lessen the chance of that happening. To do that, we must ensure that we operate from the heart or the higher self. If the reader is puzzled, they should admit it to themselves and seek greater clarity from the tarot. Asking the querent to select extra cards will often cast light upon a puzzling spread. Under no circumstances should you ever invent information, no matter how tempting that might be; to do so is unworthy of your calling.

Intuition should always rule! Magick often defies reason, and so do the workings of the tarot. It is now that the student's meditative studies and confidence in their own ability will reap dividends. The student soon will gain confidence and speak with the *inner voice*. After a time, this visionary approach becomes second nature and ceases to be fitful. Messages that come in this way are rarely anything but accurate. The reader is a medium, nothing more. It is essential to be distanced from the situation. We did not create the world; it is what it is.

Often, clients will take the reader into their confidence; never ever break that trust by discussing their personal affairs with anyone else. A tarot reader's client deserves the same right to privacy and confidentiality as someone discussing an important matter with their doctor or lawyer (with the same caveats about illegal or abusive matters). Remember, a querent gets from the tarot what they put into it. All experienced readers know that occasionally one encounters arrogance if not downright hostility from clients. Dismiss it from your mind; the loss is theirs.

The tarot also teaches us not to be too hasty in judging the actions of others. All of us have a part to play and the way in which each individual fits into the Divine Plan is depicted in the Arcana. It is a false view of existence that causes pain to our real being; thus, we should constantly appeal to be shown the truth. Virtues may easily become vices unless we always remain aware. The tarot shows us and all we need to know is how to recognise its insights.

Often, certain cards seem to attach themselves to individuals. We all reflect archetypes, and our previous lives are mirrored in our present existence. To discover what is missing in our worldview rather than reinforce what we already possess is the challenge of any incarnation. It is the balance that is most important. This does not mean that we need to undertake a constant evaluation of good and evil; that is a worthless exercise. It is the avoiding of extremes of thought or behaviour that is important. As the artist knows, *tone* matters more than colour.

Readers must realise that they are the bringers of faith, and they should share that faith with the querent. The reader will progress along their own spiritual path and realise that the power of the universe is (like The High Priestess) all-seeing and all-knowing. They are aware that the tarot is a window upon the universe, and it has the means to answer any question.

A reading reflects the occasion when it occurs. It is an exchange of energy, one that is brought about by the presence of the reader, the querent, and the tarot. Whatever stimulus prompts the querent to seek a reading is encapsulated in a unique moment. That moment triggers another—the one in which the reading takes place. The cards that appear are the ones that the querent is destined to see and to reflect upon; they are chosen by the universe. The tarot provides an understanding of one's place in the cosmos. Mouni Sadhu reflects too upon its impartial nature:

> *The tarot is neutral; neither good nor evil in itself, just like figures which can express any quantity, suitable or unsuitable, true or false. The whole system is based on the Universal Principle, which manifests itself in every sphere of life. We may call it the 'Law'.... This Law works on every plane of existence.[12]*

The tarot is a great teacher. It informs; it will tell you anything you wish to know—or what you ought to know—eventually. Like all great teachers, the cards know instinctively when any person is ready to receive a particular wisdom. We are constantly being given lessons and the tarot is a distillation of that cosmic instruction. The tarot is a vision of our world and the ongoing story of our lives; it does not exist outside the world, in a realm of make-believe.

Live with the tarot, understand it, walk in its landscapes, fly in its skies, and meet those that dwell there. It is a living world, beautiful, significant, gentle, and telling. The tarot was created to help you—accept this great gift.

---

12   Sadhu, Mouni, *The Tarot—A Contemporary Course of the Quintessence of Hermetic Occultism* (George Allen and Unwin, 1964).

CHAPTER TWO

*"We are what we think.
All that we are arises with our thoughts.
With our thoughts we make the world.
Speak or act with a pure mind
And happiness will follow you
As your shadow, unshakeable."*

—The Dhammapada

THE FOOL .

THE MAGICIAN.

THE HIGH PRIESTESS

THE EMPRESS.

The Major Arcana and
the Spheres of Understanding

The cards of the Major Arcana represent *principles* and are multi-layered in their meaning. The cards of the Minor Arcana, although equally important, refer to the more mundane details of the querent's life. The Major Trumps are a complete philosophical system in their own right. Own a tarot pack and you have before you a book of wisdom.

The Heart of Creation

The Fool, The Magician, The High Priestess, The Empress

> *"I learned to recognise the thorough and primitive duality of man; I saw that, of the two natures that contended in the field of my consciousness, even if I could rightly be said to be either, it was only because I was radically both."*
> —Robert Louis Stevenson, *Dr. Jekyll and Mr. Hyde*

The first cards we shall study are those numbered 0, I, II, and III; respectively, The Fool, The Magician, The High Priestess, and The Empress. Lay out this quartet in any combination you wish. Regard them closely until you feel their power and wisdom, for you have before you all the secrets of the universe. That is a great claim to make, you might think—too great, perhaps. Allow me to convince you! Let us look at the two male figures first—but already we should pause, for they do not represent what we traditionally associate with male figures. Is there something sprightly about The Fool, stepping over the precipice without a care in the world? The Magician, too, is youthful, with a slightly arched expression in his features. These are gods, not denizens of the earthly plane. We see them as they might wish to be seen. These two Arcana represent the active principles of magick, and I stress *active* because, as we shall discover, their female counterparts have a passive air. But nothing is quite as it seems in the world of the tarot.

The Fool is always inspired; he is the immediate instant —the "right" moment—present, tantric, elusive. He has no dealings with the past or the future, knowing that any view of time as linear is simply incorrect. Individual moments may shape an outcome, but they exist independently of each other. The Fool teaches us about time and space, demonstrating that they are one and the same. His number is 0. As one who recognizes neither past nor future and knows that time is not linear, he stands outside the linear world of numbers altogether. No calculation of any complexity that does not involve the concept of nothing is possible.[13] In the same way, we must realise that the unexpected or the unidentified can always make a surprise appearance. The Fool steps, not blindly but knowingly, from the security of the solid earth into the abyss below. The plane he enters is the abode of power, and he is one with that power already. With his leap

---

13   The mathematical conception of *zero* is an "empty place indicator" and as a concept of "nothing." Its origin was in India, from whence came the greatest mathematicians, far in advance of those of ancient Greece. The use of "zero" was not taken up in the West until the seventeenth century.

into the unknown, The Fool has become so much part of the universe that he is every part of it. The Fool is the phenomenal state challenging the causal. It seems we are constantly poised between order and anarchy. The Fool balances precariously on a cliff edge—will he jump or will he not? Will he fall to his death, or will he transcend the limited view of the physical world as ultimate reality and simply walk into another dimension? In order to answer these questions in a tarot reading, one must consider the circumstances in the querent's situation and question. Much may be gained from contemplation of the little white dog that accompanies him. Is he encouraging humanity to make a leap into the unknown, or is he barking a warning before it is too late?

The Fool has no identity; he is the phenomenal element always challenging the causal.[14] The Fool can be linked to the planet Uranus, which has an eccentric orbit and an equally bizarre vibration.[15] Like Mars and Saturn, it sometimes has a malefic influence. Yet at the same time, Uranus can give charisma to those under its influence. It can induce

---

14   Kant maintained that the perceptions of the intuitive mind were organised so as to produce experience. Defining reality by *a priori* (independent of experience) or *a posteriori* (experienced or contingent) method is a cornerstone of philosophy. Introduce the approach to reality of Castaneda's Don Juan into the debate and it becomes *very* interesting!

15   The Sun instigates light and life, while Uranus is manifest as lightning. The polarity is made even clearer when we consider that Leo (the Sun) opposes Aquarius (Uranus). In our times, the Uranian vibration manifests itself as artificial and inorganic energy. Electricity and synthesised chemicals, which are an important part of the symbolism of Uranus, are *unnatural*—a false reality. By relying so much on technology, we have become the servant of an unruly master. The relationship Uranus has with spiritual matters was demonstrated by the popularity of LSD in the 1960s. Those who indulged in this drug often mistook their heightened state of awareness for enlightenment.

creativity and insight. This is all very well until those influences go to the subject's head. Uranus has no conscience and those who are adversely influenced by the planet are often superficial and lacking in compassion.

The Fool carries in his left hand a white rose, the *Rosa Mundi*—soul of the world, the most perfect of flowers, the bloom of Eden. It sustains purity and passion, death and life.[16] The rose has an association with each of our four cards. The Empress card does not appear to possess a rose, but in the legend, Venus (the goddess represented by the card of The Empress) sprang from the sea and where the foam fell, white roses grew. The rose is a sign of paradise, expanding awareness (through the five petals representing the five senses) and suffering. In Christian iconography, it is a symbol of Mary the Queen of Heaven and Christ himself. In Syrian magic, *rose* means "secret conjurations," and words of power such as *sub rosa* mean "silence and secrecy." The Magus has often had to be discreet and secretive; The Fool not so.

The affinity between The Magician and The Fool is very apparent.[17] The Fool is the *essence of magick*—its actual power. The Magician is aware that *every* act is a magical act; that knowledge separates him from his ordinary fellows. The Fool

---

16   It appears upon the banner held by Death.

17   The Fool has a correspondence with the planet Uranus and The Magician is linked to Mercury. The former has no definite gendered presentation, the latter is androgynous. An astrologer's interpretation of how a conjunction of these two planets would manifest in an individual is a "…person who can shed new light on a situation by looking at it in a totally new way, the individual who can cut through the ambivalence, tradition, and fear and suggest a completely different alternative." See also Tompkins, Sue, *Aspects in Astrology* (Random House, 2001) p.172.

is totally balanced—in the moment—poised on the edge of the abyss. The Magician, too, has that equilibrium when he practices his art: he is poised between two worlds. Both know that the outcome of their endeavours will always be successful. They have been chosen by the Masters of the Inner Planes to bring the perfection of Heaven to the chaos of Earth. The beginner in magick often makes the mistake of denigrating the material world at the expense of the spiritual. This is a great error, for the one is only a reflection of the other.

Study the image of The Magician, standing at the altar, between the blooms of Heaven and the flowers of the earth which he has manifested. The Divine Power flows for eternity around the *lemniscate,* the symbol of infinity, above him.[18] The infinity sign is similar to a horizontal figure-eight, a number sacred in many cultures.[19] It crackles like lightning around the wand he holds aloft in his right hand, is sent through the Kabbalistic Sephiroth of Tiphareth that is the magician's heart, to emerge from the fingers of the left hand which he is pointing towards the earth, thus renewing it. He points "as above, so below"—the macrocosm and the microcosm. The slight smile that hovers around his features hints that, on one level, he is simply enjoying the experience. He is detached from what he is doing and yet totally involved—that is yet another magickal paradox, one essential to those who

---

18   This symbol is also found on the Strength card, which is the card of Leo, ruled by the Sun. The card of *The Magician* is numbered I, which in numerology is also assigned to the Sun.

19   It is the *octagram,* a symbol of regeneration in the I Ching. There are eight Pagan festivals, and the *Sun Wheel* of India has eight spokes. The figure can be aligned with a flow of energy through the chakras and is always cyclic in nature.

would understand the nature of magick. He acts with ease. To The Magician, work is play.

He has been made master of the four elements and laid out before him are the symbols of the Minor Arcana: Wands (Fire), Swords (Air), Cups (Water), and Pentacles (Earth). Quicksilver is another name for mercury, and it is through the speed of his thinking combined with his will that he creates his own reality.

Mercury is the astrological correspondence of *The Magician* card. The Latin Mercury is the same as the Greek Hermes, known to many students of the occult because of his connection with Hermetic philosophy. Hermes is a god who can travel between the worlds; he can join the other gods in the heavenly realm atop Mt. Olympus, visit with the mortals upon Earth, or descend into the Underworld, for he is the one who leads the goddess Persephone back to her mother every spring from her subterranean sojourn and who carries messages from the other gods atop Olympus down to Hades in the world below.

The Magician has the power to bring about a change in consciousness, but he remains a servant of the divine consciousness. He knows that what is often perceived as "reality" is merely various phenomena in a state of flux. This state is always capable of being rearranged. The magician works in the spaces around objects and deliberately blurs the definition between them. He knows that what is defined as reality is often a consensus, so his task is always made easier. He unerringly follows the principle that divine will exists—his power will only operate successfully if it is in harmony with the heavens. He also knows that the spirit of the Temple resides with the High Priestess, its guardian and its keeper. By combining their power in an equal exchange, the spark is created for a magickal working. In any relationship, this can be considered one of the keys to harmony, for it advocates the blending of the sexes, not a confrontation.

Polarity is essential to magick. It is not the same as *duality*, which is an intellectual error, and one that has undermined the Christian faith. Duality posits a world which has at its core two absolutes, usually defined as good and evil. In contrast, polarity is the understanding that nothing is exclusively masculine or feminine—everything contains aspects of its opposite. Thus, summer and winter are the polarities of the year, light and darkness the polarities of the day, joy and sorrow the polarities of emotion.

In the same way, every human being, regardless of their gender, contains elements of both the masculine and feminine polarities. Carl Jung taught that there is a woman within every man, a feminine half which he called the *anima*, a word meaning *soul*. She dwells in the depths of the unconscious mind and, for creative artists who have the ability to make contact with her, she acts as an inner Muse. Equally, each woman has a masculine half within her unconscious, which Jung called the *animus* and which can provide strength and purpose.

Emma Jung, Carl's wife and his "intellectual editor," also worked within the same framework. She defined the female as one who is "pre-eminently practical and applied…solving riddles…she contents herself with faith…."[20] It is said that the Garden of Eden was an allegory of the feminine. Like the Rose of Venus, as well the Morning Star and myrtle in the evening, the feminine is depicted as the essential inner spark of divinity.

Imagination and intellect will manifest in different ways, but neither quality is exclusively masculine or feminine. A man may choose to be an artist and channel his energies to celebrate beauty. The mother in defending her children may be said to be "martial," like the planet Mars, named for the ancient Roman god of war. Those beyond the gender binary may still hold both masculine and feminine qualities. The interaction between the masculine and feminine (such as in magick) causes a synthesis.

The Empress and The High Priestess respectively represent the outer and inner world of femininity. The Moon rules our feelings and our subconscious, while The High Priestess, whose astrological correspondence is the Moon,[21] owns the secrets of Isis.[22] This knowledge must be kept from the common gaze, or it may be misunderstood or reviled. It lies beyond "[t]he famous pillars of Joachin and Boaz…built for Solomon" seen in the card.[23] The High Priestess is the pure spiritual path.

---

20   Jung, Emma, "Animus and Anima: Two Essays," *Wirklichkeit der Seele* (Rascher Verlag, 1934).

21   Not the card titled The Moon, as would be supposed, and which represents Neptune.

22   Isis, as The High Priestess, is before the veil. This correspondence only existed after 1800. Prior to that, The High Priestess card was titled The Papess, an enigmatic reference to the medieval legend of a female pope or to *Fortuna*, the female aspect in the Gnostic Trinity.

23   Unknown Author

The seeker must know what lies beyond the veil to achieve their quest. Then they will be capable of making the right decisions in their earthly life. The High Priestess asks that a choice be made. How we act determines the outcome, but we must not resist change, for then our fears create a tension which will not allow energy to flow freely. The result is stagnation and sterility, leading ultimately to death. If we always allow others to choose for us, the will is rendered powerless, and our courage and tenacity disappear. Intuition and conscience help us to act in accordance with what is right. In this way, The High Priestess is a valuable ally because she knows the secrets of every one of us. By contacting this goddess energy, we access the greatest guidance.

Light and darkness are in all of us.[24] The Moon's influence is felt strongly in the crowd, turning it suddenly from a joyous throng into an ugly mob. The waxing moon determines the time of growth, the tides' ebb and flow. Water is endlessly fascinating to look upon because it is always changing, as our time should always be. If our life appears to be stale, it is because we are not looking deeply enough into its ways. We are not seeing the wonder and beauty therein. The Moon advises us as to the right time to do things—when to sow and when to reap.

The Moon is the mother, watching over us at night and secretly nurturing and protecting us by day. Her light may be cold and fragile, but it is part of the darkness, not a rival to it. The Sun's light drives away darkness; the Moon is in

---

24   Nephthys is the sister of Isis and mother of Anubis, companion of the dead. She is known as the Black Isis, the dark side of the Moon.

harmony with her solar brother. In magical terms, The Magician dares, whereas The High Priestess knows. You will notice that The Fool and The Magician are both in action, while The High Priestess and The Empress are both in repose. They have transformed the raw power of magick into something serene. Their concentration is as intense, but it has a different *modus operandi*. It would be foolish to underestimate the power of The Empress and The High Priestess as they have as much strength as The Fool and The Magician. Balance is at the heart of the tarot, as we shall see.

In the Arthurian tradition, Nimue (the Lady of the Lake) and Morgan le Fay (the Enchantress) sometimes blend into one composite figure. In the tarot they are reflected, respectively, in the Arcana of The High Priestess and Death. They are both aspects of Isis and the Moon, inexorably linked to romance.

It is significant that Isis, who holds almost a monopoly amongst goddesses in the Egyptian pantheon, features so strongly in the tarot. Isis reveals herself only to a few, and when those chosen are in her presence, they are aware that they stand before the Divine Goddess. She causes the manifestation of the material from out of the astral realms. All is in her image; all that can be seen upon the material plane is but the vision of the Goddess. The munificence—the eternal wisdom of the Goddess—is in all things. In the old packs, she was The Papess, but has since been restored to her more fitting title of The High Priestess.

Later, in Christian times, worship of the Goddess Isis was sometimes suppressed (though not entirely). But the Gnostics, the knowledge seekers who adapted Christianity to their own esoteric purposes, simply found another name for her. The High Priestess, the Goddess Isis—they are none other than Sophia, the Goddess of Wisdom.[25]

The Priestess has practised her magick in the Temple since ancient times. The most telling depiction of her resides in The High Priestess card of the tarot. Looking particularly knowing, as The Magician appears to be equally enigmatic, is the High Priestess sitting before the veil. It is a curtain decorated with a design of pomegranates and represents desire for knowledge and the netherworld simultaneously. The veil hides what is beyond, but what can just be seen in Pamela Colman Smith's masterly design is an endless stretch of water. It appears to be calm on the surface, but as we all know, beneath the waves are always powerful and mysterious, ever-changing currents. The key to every puzzle is to be found beyond the veil, as well as the way to rectify every dilemma.

The Empress is surrounded by fecundity and growth. Unlike The High Priestess, she likes to display her beauty and munificence. She bears fruit and bestows light and life. She is the natural world, the earth at its most fertile and good—the spirit of Gaia. Her astrological correspondence is the goddess of love Venus, and Venus is a benefic planet, the source of joy and pleasure, desiring always peace and harmony. But just as Venus is renowned for her free expression of sensuality, so The Empress also desires the sexual energy of The Emperor so that their union will bear fruit. There in

---

25   McCombs, Terry, *Sophia* (Internet Book of Shadows, 1999), retrieved from sacred-texts.com/bos/bos251.htm.

all seasons, ripening in the spring, sumptuous at the harvest, tender in autumn, The Empress is the power of birth, life, and regeneration. Earth spirits reside in her kingdom, where trees and stones have an inner life and all is holy. She reminds us that the earthly realm has as much spirituality as the dominions of the other elements. She wears a crown of stars to show her queenly status. The High Priestess has the halo of the Moon, The Magician is crowned with the symbol of eternity, while The Fool simply has a feather in his cap! They are all crowned with glory, for they are instruments of the divine. For our quartet to stray from the path of good and righteousness would be unthinkable and impossible.

The number of The Empress is III—the trinity—an acknowledgment of three states of being: mother, father, and child. No part of the trinity can exist without the other, thus sustaining an eternal state of change.

The Empress as the Goddess forever tests us, particularly our faith in the rightness of things. Her love is unconditional, and the Goddess expects us to be the same with her. If we are to be truly one with her, we must accept all her ways—from the terrible to the sublime. She is the mirror of the lake as well as the fathomless seas. Her love is endless and eternal, as are all her passions. Her essential goodness assigns her the title, like Isis, of "the Queen of Heaven." She has all the attributes of a great queen, having a rare beauty and great gifts of intellect and conversation. Parallels to the Empress can be found numerous times in global mythologies, such as the flower bride, Blodeuwedd, in Welsh tradition and Venus and Aphrodite in Greco-Roman myth.

Man

The Emperor, The Hierophant, The Chariot, The Hermit

> *"Chesed, the king on his throne, the father of his people in times of peace, may win our love; but it is Geburah, the king in his chariot going forth to war, who commands our respect."*
> —Dion Fortune, *Mystic Brotherhood University: Later Lessons*

Reason is highly developed in humanity.[26] It is a jealous state wishing to exclude all other means of perception. In society, reason is the foundation of judgment, and thus justice is meted out by individuals to their fellows. It is significant that the Justice card in the tarot depicts a female figure. We shall discuss this aspect of tarot symbolism in its proper place later.

Once the power of kings was absolute and omnipotent, owning the power of life and death over their subjects. It was commonly believed that the mere touch of the king could heal illness and disease. The notion of the divine right of kings still simmers in the British psyche, and tellingly, we as

---

26 David Hume, the eighteenth-century philosopher, spoke of "inductive inference," which is the belief that what we have observed happening will occur again. This inference—the principle of the uniformity of Nature—succeeds only with reference to logic itself. In understanding, reason will often win out, but magick demonstrates dramatically that it can also fall at the first fence.

THE EMPEROR.

THE HIEROPHANT

THE CHARIOT.

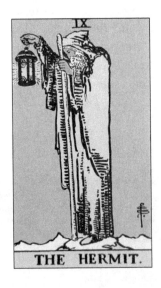

THE HERMIT.

a nation never trust our politicians.[27] If we deny the power within us, we obstruct nature and ignore our destiny. It will find us out in the end, so it is better that we realise the good we can achieve with our mental and physical strength. Much abuse of power results from insecurity. The ego wishes to maintain a status quo. If it succeeds, it limits understanding because it makes for an unbalanced perception.

The true Martial type is dynamic but also controlled. He is a master of the Fire within, making him even-tempered and patient under provocation. The warrior maintains his impeccability at the expense of everything else. Like the magician, he keeps aloof from the doings of the world. As the Buddhists tell us: "Be *in* the world, but not *of* it." Warrior kings were the first rulers of men. A leader who was more than simply "a chief among the mighty" could discipline his own heart and mind. In that way, he gained enlightenment and served his people.

The Emperor represents the highest earthly power. Not surprisingly, he is associated with the sign of Aries, shown by the rams' heads on his throne. No moral principle is inherent here; the Emperor represents the power of life and

---

27   Good kings and bad kings there have been, with a slight bias towards the former. Although the idea of a republic with its democratic overtones still seems attractive to many, the *romance* of kingship never lessens. John Michel, in his *Confessions of a Radical Traditionalist* (Inner Traditions International, 2015), remarks that "[a] president may be a very respectable and worthy person, but countries under a president rather than a king and queen are constitutionally second rate. Even little girls know that, for they are natural princesses and are entitled to marry handsome princes rather than the uncouth sons of Chairman Somebody. Poetically and spiritually, kings are real whereas presidents are merely human conventions."

holds the ankh, the Egyptian symbol of vitality.[28] His physical energy will eventually dwindle and, in the Death card, he surrenders to the inevitable. In his heart, The Emperor knows he owns only temporal power. The Emperor wears his armour beneath his cloak and is always ready to take up arms, hopefully for the right.

Mars, the ruler of Aries, is the planet of action and resolution. Martial energy is always seen and felt. Traditionally, a king holds the world (the orb) in one hand and the symbol of his power over it (the sceptre) in the other. He makes decisions and expects his envoys to carry them out. Originally an agrarian god, Mars' role was to rid the crops of pestilence. His transformation into a God of War may have coincided with the Age of Aries beginning in 2000 BCE. This age superseded the previous Age of Taurus, a matriarchal era.

By serving their king, his subjects imbue him with energy. It is to be hoped that this power is used well, for a monarch does not always possess the virtue of temperance. The Emperor is a man of reason, not easily swayed in his opinion, and inclined to the coldest of logic. With him, there is little middle ground; his views are black and white, not necessarily narrow-minded, but always single-minded. He is the father, just and protective, but when his energy is misdirected, he becomes the tyrant. He may be violent and sanguine, and the negative side of The Emperor is only too apparent in the many conflicts that continue to erupt on this planet.

---

28   The ankh is also the symbol of Isis, who is associated with the Water sign of Cancer. A magical polarity of Fire and Water exists here.

The number of The Emperor is IV. It is the first number that can be factorised. It forms the square, which in turn becomes the cube. In this Arcanum, structure is born. However, straight lines restrict and enclose—four is *rigid*. Its limitations are in its very weight and purpose. The number of The Hierophant is V. Five is deemed to be unstable because it is a combination of odd and even elements and thus constantly in motion. All the fives in the Minor Arcana depict a difficult phase in life. The Hierophant strives to make order from chaos, champions the subduing of the physical self, and thus the elevation of the soul. His power comes from above, like The Magician, but The Hierophant directs and enforces this power not toward the earth, but onto his disciples.

The Hierophant is associated with the sign of Taurus, fixed and earthy. He and The Emperor represent, respectively, the Church and the State—a common but uneasy alliance. Our own age sees the struggle between the dictator and the fundamentalist, both equally repellent. The priesthood is as hierarchical as the world of politics, and neither will ever be free of intrigue and ambition. Both depend for their survival on the willingness of their followers to submit to a particular creed. Unquestioning belief is at the heart of any *theocracy*, a system of governing which only exists because people often yearn to be told what to think—it makes life easier. To trust implicitly in man's definition of God is unwise. The Hierophant imposes discipline, which is no bad thing, but when the desire for order degenerates into bigotry, it is to be deplored.

The Chariot is the other lunar card in the deck, and the black and white images echo The High Priestess. Its number is VII (traditionally lucky), which represents the mystery of the universe. The astrological correspondence is with Cancer, the sign of the Mother who is capable of fighting tooth and nail to protect her offspring and her home. Pamela Colman Smith has deliberately made the art sexually ambiguous. Originally, this card was entitled Victory and was notably feminine in nature. Perhaps this reflected the idea that Victory is not to be equated with celebration. War is always repugnant in the eyes of widows and grieving mothers.

Emotion is the motif of this Arcanum and, more than that, the ability to control one's feelings—a necessity and a sign of a stable character. Any rush of unrestrained emotion can be as destructive to the psyche as an avalanche or a flood in the physical domain. Cloying sentiment is as weakening as unbridled anger; either can overwhelm the senses and blind reason.

The Charioteer has a talent for creating illusions. He is the actor whose words move the crowd, the conjurer at whose tricks we marvel. So comfortable is he in his domain of mist and shadows that he sometimes fails to notice when others are lost or out of their depth. Even when they are drowning, he may leave them to their fate. In his dark mood, he is as cold and lifeless as the Moon. This is the card of Diana the Huntress or Athena the warrior queen. Do not be taken in by the glamour surrounding The Chariot; its wheels have the power to crush those who are foolish enough to stray into its path.

To be alone is often a blessing; to be lonely is a curse. The Hermit may appear to be isolated, but as the guardian of the eternal light, he is sustained through times of darkness and doubt. The Hermit represents the sign of Virgo. Prudence is his virtue, for he is the reflective side of Mercury. He is The Magician in his passive and covert role, isolated from the world, as the magickal calling is not conducive to society and the social whirl. Sharing experience is a definite need for most *Homo sapiens;* we seek to refer to each other, but magicians, as a rule, do not yearn for the company of others. The light in The Hermit's lamp will never be extinguished, for it is the light of truth; its owner dares to search for truth through the state of solitude. Though he sometimes becomes melancholy, The Hermit will never surrender completely to despair. He continues along his way though it may be one of silence and darkness. No desire or possibility of change enters his awareness; he is aware only of his next footstep. The number of the card is IX, made up of three times three, a dynamic combination associated with movement but here manifesting as constancy.

The Hermit makes an appearance in our collective myths upon occasion. Take, for example, Merlin, the great magician of the Arthurian mythos; his situation was quite extreme, for he found himself lonely and isolated. Perhaps his state was even more acute because he knew he could gain no solace from the love or friendship of any mortal. As a seer, Merlin is renowned for his magickal staff, which sometimes gives him the appearance of The Hermit in the tarot. The staff has an equal power to the wand, and both have been a badge of office since ancient times. Hermes owns the caduceus, while the loop of the ankh is held by the gods of ancient Egypt and is the symbol of life. It also represents the combined power of Isis and Osiris, the womb and lingam combined. Thoth, the god of magick, holds his staff with the same authority that Merlin will come to do in another era. There is much to link these two figures. They both represent will made manifest and tempered by the presence of the universe.

There is another lonely wanderer upon the path of knowledge and magic who walks through the world cloaked in grey and carrying a staff. This is the god Odin, the highest of the gods in Norse mythology. But despite his heavenly seat, high upon a great mountain where he may study the world below him in all its glory and its tragedy, he sometimes chooses to appear in the world of the mortals, where he wanders as a white-bearded old man with his staff; like other Hermit-like figures, wherever he goes, magick follows, magick is made.

Knowledge

The Lovers, The Hanged Man, Death, The Devil

> *"Knowledge is really confined to experience. The laws of nature are, as Kant said, the laws of our minds, and, as Huxley said, the generalization of observed facts."*
> —Aleister Crowley

As the Sun is at the centre of our galaxy, love is light, and light is at the heart of love. If we give love and know love,

THE LOVERS.

THE HANGED MAN.

DEATH.

THE DEVIL.

we walk in the most exalted realms. "God is Love" is no trite slogan; it is an expression of divine nature. It is the wish to be that fuels the universe. The universal mind is, in the Hegelian sense, the notion of all being related to all. In contemplating this idea, we must remember that the mind and the brain are not the same thing. The brain is an organ like any other in the body; the mind is the name we give to that state of consciousness we experience. How we see the world determines how we manifest the world. If our vision always comes from the heart, then we may be assured that love will always colour our lives.

Recall again Hermes' caduceus, the magical staff that could answer any question. Its design is that of two serpents, and the Arcanum known as The Lovers represents *union*. This is the card of Gemini—the twins—and ruled by Mercury, the planet of magick and intellect. An angel presides over a choice made, perhaps between the sacred and the profane. The original title of the card was "Vice and Virtue," and its lesson is to always have a pure motive.[29] Clarity of purpose is always to be found in the heart; the mind often deludes itself.

The Lovers is numbered VI, representing the next stage of perfection after four. The balance of the number six is more sophisticated than the two of The High Priestess or the simple four of The Emperor. Six signifies gain and advancement through experience and genuine goodwill. Gemini is associated with the child, and the vision of a

---

29   It contained an extra figure, another woman. The scenario involved the youth choosing a virtuous partner—or not, perhaps?

child is untainted by shadows and malice. It is the compromises we choose to make that can spoil our unfettered joy.

In The Lovers, the affection that first began with The Empress continues to flow. Endless and unrestrained without any desire to control, love brings peace and comfort to all sentient creatures. Without it, our lives are barren and meaningless. Love is a miracle; the greatest gift creation can bestow upon us.

All true love must be selfless. The sacrifice that is made at the altar of love is that of the self. The role of the priest is always a sacrificial one, as they will undergo the fires of redemption in the name of their calling. They must be ruthless with any imperfections in their own character yet forgiving of the weaknesses they may detect in others. They are aware that all upon the earthly plane is composed of illusion, and for this reason, they have learned from their divine masters that they should not judge. If nothing exists, then there is nothing to judge! The theme of abandonment in this Arcanum contrasts strongly with the charioteer in The Chariot, who deliberately reins in any wild tendencies.

The soul of humanity yearns for peace and wisdom, and only the Divine can provide that sublime state. The Arcanum of this principle is The Hanged Man. The card has a link to the Water sign Pisces. While Christ represents the Age of Pisces, the figure depicted in the card is probably of an earlier era. It could be Odin, who hung himself upon the World Tree of Yggdrasil to realise the secret of the runes. To renounce the material plane for the transcendental and test the soul is an ecstatic principle, with the goal of traveling between the worlds.

To understand the ideas presented here, much will be gained from examining the imagery of this most enigmatic of the cards of the tarot. The state in which the apparently contented figure finds himself, or chooses to be in, is between two worlds. He is secured to his earthly support yet free to float in the aether. On his joining with the element of Air, he gains wings and flies. He is carried high, inspiration keeping him above the mountains, until, like Icarus, he eventually falls. Now he must encounter the change that will accompany his entry into the world of Fire. With his newfound illumination, he is purified and transformed. His great energy, as if riding a mighty steed into the Sun, is like a magickal death and leads him to the next element in the chain.

The Hanged Man does not struggle against his fate; he willingly surrenders to it. He appears to possess no will and is thus also the antithesis of The Emperor.[30] It would be more pertinent to conclude that his will has been transformed and become part of the divine will. The Hanged Man is like a follower of Zen or a poet. He is the mystic, never the magician. In his negative aspect, he is the drifter, the vagabond, or the drunkard. Content with having no purpose or responsibility, he is an outcast from society and often prefers to remain so.

Although we might regard death as the cessation of life—non-being as opposed to being—is this all? Certainly, death is associated with tragedy for those who remain and carry the loss of a loved one, but Death itself is not a tragic figure. Life is a series of births and deaths, and in realizing

---

30   Aries (The Emperor) is the first sign of the zodiac, Pisces the end of the cycle of twelve.

the nature of death, we gain more understanding of life. Throughout the centuries, both Death and Time are depicted carrying a scythe—perhaps death is the price one pays to exist in time. The tarot card of Death is numbered XIII. Using that lateral addition so essential to the numerologist, the number XIII is reduced to IV—The Emperor. The astrologer would see this as a correspondence between Aries and Scorpio (The Emperor and Death respectively), both traditionally ruled by Mars.

Those born under Scorpio are secretive and conceal from the world their deepest feelings. Emotions run at their most intense here, from loyalty and total surrender to ruthlessness and revenge. Injure a scorpion and you will be struck down mercilessly when you least expect it. A monarch rules through death—they succeed to their position at the death of the last king or queen and holds the power of life and death over their subjects.

Death is the most valuable teacher we have! Nothing which has ever occurred on Earth has made the slightest difference to the universe at large. Thus, we might suggest that nothing anybody says or does has any significance! Understand that and you will develop a love for the world as great as if you were personally its creator. For the artist, it is enough to create. The true artist knows that art lies in *the act*, not the result. The end of a life means nothing to life itself. The Sun still rises, the birds continue to sing, and the stars do not fall from the sky. Our own brief sojourn has ended; that is all. That knowledge should strengthen and reassure us of the very rightness of things. A greater attachment to the universe occurs when it is realised that the self is transparent. The individual presence may be felt but is really invisible.

Life resides with the self, Death with the non-self. To regard Death as the agency of the divine is the beginning of wisdom. We may cheat death once or maybe even twice, but it always wins in the end. It is not its nature to rejoice in victory, even though in war it knows it is always the only winner. But Death, like The Magician, is distant from the affairs of humans. Death wears the red plume of The Fool, another figure who stands outside of the world. The white rose on Death's banner is too the same flower that The Fool holds. Is the Sun in the background of the Death card rising or setting? It does not matter—time is an illusion. Better to regard existence as an endless series of changes than a tedious progression of the hours. When we cease to fear death, we are able to see that all the changes in our lives are part of a constantly changing cycle. As something within us dies, something else is reborn. Death is not an end; it is a beginning.

Look again at The Hierophant and place this card next to The Devil. Do you notice the similarity between them? Astrologically, they are both assigned to the element of Earth (Taurus and Capricorn, respectively). Religion is a force that holds many in its sway, but The Devil too has an influence that cannot be ignored. The two figures attached to the cube of his throne can slip their chains at any time, but they willingly choose to remain there. Is their devotion the same as the figures kneeling before The Hierophant?

We assume not, believing their addiction to Evil is misdirected energy. No salvation exists in The Devil's domain; it is a place of barrenness and cynicism. It is a place where no hope or joy resides and the souls there remain empty and wretched.

Physical ailments are a sign that the aetheric body has been weakened. When this occurs, the aura darkens and is torn. Temptation comes to us when our will is weak. Then, we may act in ways that later our conscience will tell us were harmful and wrong. We are constantly tested—more so the closer we are to our spiritual goal. We must trust the divine, for once we deny that protection, we are lost. The Devil desires us, like Faustus, to turn our back on the angels and think only of ourselves.

The outsider and outcast Lucifer is the fallen angel, which gives a more romantic cast to the picture. William Blake wrote in his poem "Proverbs of Hell" that "[t]he lust of the goat is the glory of God," and indeed, Pan or Cernunnos, the Lord of Animals, is the nature god. In this incarnation, the Saturnine element seems altogether more attractive. He will still frighten us when he leaps out of the wildwood, but he is not *sinister,* simply a spirit of the earth. Priapic Pan is bursting with unbridled sexuality and taunts the prude and the puritan. The Church stigmatised the Pagan way, but, ironically, Paganism is now a flourishing faith in the New Age.

THE STAR.

THE MOON.

THE SUN.

The Heavens

The Star, The Moon, The Sun

> *"Our birth is but a sleep and a forgetting:*
> *The Soul that rises with us, our life's Star."*
> —William Wordsworth,
> "Ode on Intimations of Immortality
> from Recollections of Early Childhood"

Stars have many associations. We wish upon a star and hope we have a lucky star. Aleister Crowley announced that "every man and every woman is a star."[31] Humankind is said to be the crown of creation. The Arcanum entitled The Star is linked to the sign of Aquarius, the sign of humanity.[32] In the background is the ibis, the symbol of Thoth, the Egyptian god of wisdom and magick. The image upon the card is of a naked, beautiful woman who seeks, by means of healing, to bring about redemption for the world. The star above, the light of the heavens that inspires it, is one of compassion. It shines upon each and every one of us, no matter how diverse our creed or culture. This is truly the spirit of the New Age which, at its true heart, promotes an all-embracing liberality.

The Magi followed the star in the heavens hoping to discover the whereabouts of the newly born Messiah. The Star is the manifestation of humans as divine, using their

---

31   Crowley, Aleister, *Liber AL vel Legis* (A∴A∴, 1909).
32   The correspondence between The Star—Aquarius and the opposite sign of Leo (Strength)—is worth investigating. The contrasting appearance yet similar demeanour of the figures should be contemplated.

intelligence and invention only for good. They seek to alleviate the sufferings and tribulations of others through their insights. The spirit of The Star embodies both tradition and change, as for its own advancement humanity must continually review and re-envision its ways and its collective goals. Humankind is still want only destroying the planet, but one can only hope that they now realise what it truly means to be a denizen of Earth. In this, our Aquarian Age, we must tread carefully if we are to survive. The Hierophant promotes conformity as a virtue; The Star champions the need of the individual for fulfilment. As with The Fool, if one is true to oneself, one can never be deceived.[33]

The card of The Moon is deceptive, even in its title, for its correspondence is not with the earth's satellite, but with the planet Neptune. There resides the kingdom of mist and deception. Though Neptune at its best can bring inspiration, creativity, and spiritual experience, it is all too often a place of nightmares and imaginings; it exists to test the initiate's fortitude in dealing with his worst fears.

In the Arthurian tales, a location such as the Forest of Broceliande becomes a representation of the unconscious mind where the most fearful monsters reside. It is like the scene depicted on the Moon card, where the initiate must pass between the pylon gates, his gaze fixed firmly on the road ahead no matter what he may sense is lying in wait for him in the shadows. Eventually, he gains the hills beyond. Even there he may encounter further challenges, but at least

---

33   Presumably one's higher self.

he has passed the first test. It seems that we must know Hell in order to experience Heaven.

In this awful place, the lowest elemental spirits reside.[34] Love has become pain and bitterness, existence destructive and joyless. Our feelings have run away from us; they send us where they will, into darker and darker terrors. We have lost our bearings; we have nothing to hold onto. There is no Earth; neither is there any sky. We only see a distorted version of everything. Doubt threatens to become our banner; we feel sorry for ourselves and wrap the cloak of despair around us for comfort.

The same two towers that appear in the Death card are here, but without the reassuring sight of the Sun behind them. The path leads into the interminable distance, but we know we must venture there. It requires great spiritual strength to journey to the other side of this card. I would recommend prayer, for oneself and for the wraiths that obstruct the way. Love and prayer will always give us protection.

The Sun is the centre of our physical and spiritual universe, the source of life. It is almost as if this great star reassures us of our actual existence. Only by the grace of the Sun's light and warmth do we continue to be, and the Sun is the centre of our being. In astrology, the position of the Sun in a natal chart indicates the conscious sense of self and the part that it plays in life. One of the lessons of The Sun is to love yourself for what you are; you cannot begin to love others until you do

---

34   Ghosts, wraiths, and zombies inhabit the lower astral plane. It is this world that is often contacted inadvertently by mediums and continually (though they may not be aware of it) by those who use drugs.

so. The Sun is the heart of the universe and in our own hearts is where love resides.

People have been worshipping the Sun for many millennia and this great, golden orb still has an unaccountable influence over both our outer and inner lives. It is necessary for our existence, and without its presence there would be no life in the solar system. It is a small wonder that the Sun represents divine power and has, since ancient times, been adopted as a symbol of earthly dominion. In Egypt, the pharaohs were blessed and were thought to become as Ra, the Sun God. In the Western tradition, the Sun is a symbol of kingship both outwardly and within. The deities Apollo, Phoebus, and Mithras are akin to mortal heroes. Christ is Mithraic, as is King Arthur. Their light dispels darkness and doubt, and all peoples benefit from their presence. The Mithraic presence is an embodiment of the axiom that beauty is truth. The Sun heals us, shows us who we are, and brings love into our lives. Mercury and Venus are so close to the Sun in our galaxy that the qualities of both planets reflect his goodness.

A child has an unquestioning love for the world, seeing it as ideal and innocent. The child in the Sun card has the feather of The Fool in his hair—innocence and rightness in all. We are all born into a state of innocence, as Wordsworth wrote: "But trailing clouds of glory do we come."[35] As the children of Heaven, the eternal soul of the universe, we should strive to maintain our pure nature. By not being

---

35   Wordsworth, William, "Ode on Intimations of Immortality from Recollections of Early Childhood," *Poems, In Two Volumes* (1807).

inhibited or feeling restricted, the artist flourishes. Creation inspires creativity. The vitality of the world, animals, trees, mountains, and rivers are echoed in the praise and devotions of humanity. It is our oneness with the Creator that makes us feel truly part of creation and in harmony with all.

The Sun is a perfect symbol for the blissful state of the Buddha in his oneness and eternity, and for the consciousness of all the other enlightened ones who have come to teach us the path to self-realization. In his youth, Merlin was mythically linked with the Sun card of the tarot: he was the innocent child astride the horse of intelligence. He did not hold onto the horse's mane to save himself, for he was all-trusting.

Wyrd

The Wheel of Fortune, The Tower, The World

"Walk the good path, the path of Spirit—between the worlds.
Be ready for the opening to the next.
Take any way you can to get on this road."
—White Bear

In contrast to the "inexorable fate" of the ancient Greeks, *Wyrd* (Old English, Saxon *wurd*, Old High German *Wurt*, Old Norse *urur)* proposes that our personal and ancestral past affects us continuously. Every choice we make in the present builds upon choices we have made before; this results in Wyrd being not the end, but the constant. "Active fate" might be one way of looking at it. Ancient peoples did

WHEEL ᴏꜰ FORTUNE.

THE TOWER.

THE WORLD.

not consider time as linear and thus regarded the universe as phenomenal rather than causal. If a person is doomed, nothing can save them, yet courage might tip the scales for an undoomed mortal. "Fortune favours the bold," as the old saying goes.

The Wheel of Fortune is an allegory of events as they happen. It is linked with Jupiter, the benefic planet, hinting that the outcome of events is always for the best.[36] The Wheel shows the ups and downs of human affairs, fortunate and less so. Those who rail against change are at odds with the universe, for the only constant thing in our lives is change. We must always be ready to accept what happens, not constantly wishing for something else to be. Not to react to pain or pleasure is the way of the *Tao*. Know compassion and distance in your dealings with others. Become as the Buddha…all seeing, all knowing.

How we see The World is our *consciousness*. We might go further and see the soul's truth—the macrocosm and the microcosm. As William Blake has it:

> *To see all the world in a grain of sand,*
> *And heaven in a wild flower,*
> *Hold infinity in the palm of your hand,*
> *And eternity in an hour.*[37]

With the shedding of all illusion comes the clear light of truth and the world as beautiful and commanding as it really is.

---

36   *"Onem bonam prorsus esse* (all fortune is certainly good)." —Boethius
37   Blake, William, *Auguries of Innocence.*

This card is linked to the planet Saturn, traditionally a limiting influence, but here representing the perfected existence. Astrologically, Saturn represents the delays and obstacles that we encounter as we attempt to walk the path to realization, but The World card reveals the blessings that Saturn may bestow upon us if we learn to deal with and overcome these challenges—clarity, inner strength, command of the world around us, confidence and authority. Every atom is blessed and has its part to play, whether it makes a blade of grass or an elephant. The eternal laws of the universe reign supreme. We have only to ask the cosmos in the right way and everything will be given to us.

Once known as the House of God, The Tower depicts a state of imbalance. That state cannot continue; divine intervention steps in and equilibrium is restored. If this upsets the affairs of humanity, so be it. Much of what is created by humanity is built upon foundations which have no spiritual substance. Material security, as earthly power, is an illusion; all can be swept away at any time.

Sudden change is associated with the planet Mars, the force that none can resist. Because this transformation is ordained from above, it also denotes illumination. Our view of the world is altered. It may be painful at the time, but it is cathartic—a spiritual cleansing. Mars is the will, that element in our existence that cannot be denied. Because we are human beings, we have free will. The possibility that we may outwit our destiny cannot be entirely dismissed!

The Virtues

Strength, Justice, Temperance, Judgment

> *"The records are impressed on a substance called akasha…*
> *in Hindu mysticism this akasha is thought to be the primary*
> *principle of nature from which the other four natural*
> *principles, fire, air, earth and water, are created."*
> —A.G.H.

In the Minchiate tarot deck, there were ninety-seven cards with many of them functioning as allegories such as Love, Time, and so on. In the eighteenth century, the Count de Gebelin recorded details of a pack that included titles such as Travel, Loss, Illness, and Disagreement. Some of these images resembled emblems, a tradition of illustrating moral lessons. The Hermit was originally titled "Prudence" and might have been the other member of this group if I had not chosen to ally him with the human figures. For my purposes, I have chosen to include Judgment here for reasons which will soon become clear. Strength, Justice, and Temperance are all depicted as female figures, although the angel of Temperance is in accordance with the nature of such supernatural beings, neither male nor female.

The Strength card shows us a beautiful woman, crowned with the lemniscate and subduing a lion. The lesson is to master one's fears in the same way that Temperance encourages us to control our inner passions. The presence of the lion in this card indicates a correspondence with the sign of Leo. Unlike the fire of Aries that drives The Emperor, it is divine

STRENGTH.

JUSTICE .

TEMPERANCE.

JUDGEMENT.

force that enables the beast to be so easily subdued. The fitness of the action is all-important, the divine will being often mysterious but always right. Often the hand of Heaven may make only a slight gesture, but it will always have far-reaching consequences. When victory is snatched from the jaws of defeat, such a power is present. It enables humans to survive in the most terrible conditions and give unshakeable resolution to those who fight for right and truth. The card is numbered VIII—solidity or even solidarity. It is two cubed. In the Minor Arcana, the cards numbered eight have the motto "never give up."

Justice is linked to the sign of Libra—the balance. The figure is not blindfolded, as she would be if earthly law were being considered. Here, the eyes are open, all-seeing, denoting divine justice. As the Egyptian god Thoth weighs the soul after death to decide its worth, so Justice evaluates what she sees before her and then makes a decision. She does not act but *reacts,* and in doing so guards the principle of equilibrium. Like The High Priestess who sits between the pillars of *Joachin* (Will) and *Boaz* (Providence), her role is to re-establish the balance between the individual and the universal. The figure of Justice holds the sword of truth, a representation of divine truth rather than earthly law. Swords signify the element Air, and all communications using words. Reason is a powerful force, but as we shall see when we study the Minor Arcana, swords can also cause pain, as they may be used for good or evil. Justice airs her views boldly and her sense of fairness is rarely in question. Sometimes, we ourselves must be the instrument of justice. It may be our destiny to rid the world of some evil, even that which might be in ourselves.

Three of the tarot cards depict an angel: The Lovers, Judgment, and Temperance. In the last of this trio, spirit and matter, the conscious and the unconscious, and even traditional ideas of the male and female are represented. Temperance is linked to the sign of Sagittarius, the centaur —half human, half beast, yet another polarity. The symbol of Fire is on the breast of the angel. This is not the Divine Fire of the Strength card or the blood heat of The Emperor; it is the warmth of optimism and generosity. It is the hallmark of the artist and the musician, those who strive to depict the world in allegory and symbol. They create colour and movement for the delight and inspiration of humanity. Temperance is the free spirit, unshackled by "can't," transported into the realm of metaphysics.

We are all subject to the laws of *karma*. The card of Judgment implies that we will eventually be assessed according to our works. The Eastern way teaches that we will return again and again until we have learned fully the lessons necessary for us. Only then will we have worked out our karma to the full and be free to enter Nirvana—paradise.

The card is associated with Pluto, the planet of secrets. At our death, all that is deep in our soul will be revealed. In that moment, we will cease to be, our personality being obliterated. We have all had different personalities, as many as we can imagine and some we cannot. We are attracted to some people and repelled by others; this reaction determined by unconscious memory. To understand ourselves more fully we should recall these past lives, for our purpose in this life is determined by what has gone before. Some of our previous experiences may have been extremely harrowing, but insight is not gained without some pain. The time when we understand that "to know all is to forgive all" is a profound moment.

If we refer constantly to the Higher Self, we will be upheld by faith. Judgment is The Will of God. That Will has decreed the human form to be merely a vehicle for the eternal spirit. The self can always be left behind, but the soul continues to be, for it has no attachment to time or place. Life is mysterious and miraculous—in death, that connection is made once more.

CHAPTER THREE

"We live in the midst of invisible forces whose effects alone we perceive. We move among invisible forms whose actions we very often do not perceive at all, though we may be profoundly affected by them."

—Dion Fortune, *Psychic Self-Defense*

THE MINOR ARCANA

Having dealt with the Major Arcana, fifty-six other cards still remain. These make up the Minor Arcana.

I cannot emphasise enough the importance of the number attributed to each Minor Arcana card. The table of correspondences at the end of the book sets out the associations connected to the numbers. The student will see patterns of meaning if they group the cards according to number. Assembling the Major Arcana according to astrological correspondence has already been mentioned. The tarot is founded upon a perceptible order, but its reasoning must always be leavened with intuition.

The four "suits"—Wands, Swords, Cups, and Pentacles—are respectively the elements Fire, Air, Water, and Earth. And as we shall see, on a more esoteric level, they are also mythically connected with the four Hallows or four treasures of the Holy Grail, among other mythological imagery worldwide.

The Spheres of Understanding

The Four Elements

Wands: Fire

Fire leaps into action; each new fire we light is a new birth. The Wands represent a suit of beginnings and of the energy and activity which accompanies them. The element of Fire, when manifest, is the Will when combined with courage and nobility. Fire is active, creative, and enthusiastic. In general, cards from the Suit of Wands tend to be positive, promising excitement in one's life. But be careful of going too far too fast, as fire can burn you.

Cups: Water

Water is the element which symbolizes human emotions. The element of Water is an ocean of silence, communicating through the heart. Sometimes we rejoice at the appearance of cards from the Suit of Cups, for they represent our greatest emotional desires and most heartfelt wishes. At other times we may feel depressed with certain cards from the Suit of Cups, for they may show us the pain and sorrow which we sometimes feel emotionally. It is important to remember that the Cups are also an expression of our love. If we love others unconditionally, we reflect the greatest virtue of Water.

Swords: Air

Most people feel trepidation when a number of Swords appear in a reading. Many of them do seem, at least upon first acquaintance, to be negative, dark, and fearsome. It should be remembered that the astrological meaning of Air is "thinking" or "intellect," and the suit of Swords provides us with a symbolic warning that many of the negative or dark elements which appear in our lives are created by the mind itself. On the positive side, the sword represents the sharp and often deadly blow—the quick response which, like a sudden decision of the mind, may often be precisely what is required in a difficult situation. Away from the more obvious associations of combat, the sword speaks to us of the honed edge of incisive thinking. Decisions are made swiftly and with confidence. It is essential for the warrior, as it is for the king, to own this quality.

Pentacles: Earth

Here in the suit of Pentacles, we meet with the material world: the earth itself, its seasons, and its ups and downs. This suit deals largely with practical matters and worldly concerns, whether fortunate or challenging. Often, the Pentacles represent financial gains and losses, as well as what those financial statuses do to our thoughts and actions. And yet, like the other suits, the worldly does not preclude spirituality or imaginative thinking. We must be willing to sit with nature and the earth to experience its fullest potential.

Let us take another look at these four suits of the Minor Arcana, for there is much more to be said about it.

The Esotericism of the Minor Arcana

Typically, we tend to see the Minor Arcana as having less magical and mystical significance than the Major Arcana, which is clearly a universal language and deeply philosophical. And yet the Minor Arcana also has its esoteric side, which extends beyond the four elements and reaches deep into the ancient recesses of mythology.

The Treasures of the Tuatha Dé Danann

The four suits of the Minor Arcana can be found throughout many cultures and lores, but it comes up pertinently in the very early in the lore of the British Isles. Here, they correspond to the four treasures of the Tuatha Dé Danann celebrated in the Irish Mythological Cycle.

Tuatha Dé Danann means "the folk of the goddess Danu." Irish mythology presents them as kings, queens, druids, bards, warriors, heroes, healers, and craftsmen with extraordinary magical powers. Though they now dwell in the Otherworld, they continue to interact with humans and our human world. They are said to live in the *sídhe,* the ancient burial mounds which dot the British Isles and which serve as entrances to Otherworld realms. In time, they became known as the *aes sidhe,* the sídhe-folk or "fairies" of later Celtic tradition.

The tales of the Tuatha Dé Danann cross paths with the Minor Arcana of the tarot when we consider the four treasures that these magical folk brought with them when they arrived in Ireland. These were the Spear of Lugh (Wands), the Sword of Light of Nuada (Swords), Dagda's Cauldron (Cups), and the Stone of Fal (Pentacles).

The Spear of Lugh

Lugh, the heroic warrior of the Tuatha Dé Danann, possessed a number of magical items. The most famous of them was his spear, which, according to the ancient Celtic legends, was said to be impossible to overcome. He also possessed a magical incantation called *Ibar*, which means "yew tree" and which made all his spear casts hit their mark. Yew was one of the most favoured woods from which to fashion weapons because of its hardness and consequent strength. He possessed yet another incantation called *Athibar* (meaning "yew again") which caused the spear to magically return to him after it had been cast. The tip of the spear had to be kept immersed in a pot of water to keep it from igniting into flames because of its extraordinary power. In the tarot, the Spear of Lugh corresponds to the Suit of Wands.

The Sword of Nuada

Nuada had been the king of the Tuatha Dé Danann for seven years before he and his people came to Ireland. He lost an arm in combat with the armies of the Fir Bolg and was therefore no longer eligible to act as king of the Tuatha Dé Danaan. In time, he fell in battle once again, beheaded by a giant with a baleful eye. His magic sword is said to be one of the four treasures of the Tuatha Dé Danaan. Not surprisingly, it corresponds to the suit of Swords in the Minor Arcana.

The Cauldron of the Dagda

The legends describe the Dagda, one of the Tuatha Dé Danann, as a figure of immense strength and power. He possessed a magic cauldron which was called the *coire ansic,* "the un-dry cauldron," which was said to be bottomless, and no man who drank from it was ever left unsatisfied. It was said to have a ladle so big that two people could fit in it.

The Cauldron of the Dagda remains alive and well in Irish folklore. Christianity transformed it into St. Brigid's pantry, which never runs out of food.

There are a number of other cauldrons in Celtic myth as well. Among the best known is the Cauldron of Cerridwen, tended by a witch but tasted by Taliesin—who may have been a genuine historical figure—who then became a powerfully inspired Bardic poet. A similar cauldron is mentioned in the old Welsh poem *Preiddeu Annwn,* which describes King Arthur's journey to the Otherworld. Some sources claim that this poem was written by Taliesin himself. In another work from Celtic Wales, the epic *Mabinogion,* King Bran is said to have possessed a magic cauldron which could restore the dead to life. Slain warriors were tossed into the cauldron to rise again. The Cauldron of the Dagda corresponds to the suit of Cups in the Minor Arcana.

The Stone of Fal

The Stone of Fal is a stone which still exists at the Inauguration Mound on the Hill of Tara in County Meath, Ireland, the mystic center of Ireland from which the four kingdoms of the four directions take their point of origin. It served as the coronation stone for the King of Tara and, hence, High King of Ireland. It is also known as the Stone of Destiny or Speaking Stone.

There are various legends in Irish myth which tell how the Stone of Fal was brought to Ireland. *The Book of Invasions,* written down in the eleventh century but containing ancient material, states that it was brought to the island long ago by the Tuatha Dé Danann.

The *Dindsenchas,* a text which chronicles the many sacred sites of Ireland, records a tradition which asserts that the Stone of Fal would roar with anger in the presence of a false king who pretended to hold dominion over Ireland. But when a rightful High King of Ireland put his feet upon it, the stone was said to roar with joy rather than anger. The stone is also said to have had the power to rejuvenate the king and endow him with a long and fruitful reign. The Stone of Fal corresponds to the suit of Pentacles in the Minor Arcana.

The Grail Hallows

It was Jessie Weston, in her book *From Ritual to Romance,* who first recognized that the four treasures of the Grail, so often described in the tales of King Arthur, were in fact founded in Celtic myths about the four treasures of the Tuatha Dé Danann. The Grail Myth is a fascinating blend of Celtic mythology and Christian mysticism, an expression of the medieval mind and its inner mystical longings. Because the treasures of the Grail correspond to the four treasures of the Tuatha Dé Danaan, they likewise have their correspondences to the four elements and therefore to the four suits of the Minor Arcana as well. In a sense, the four Grail Hallows may be said to exemplify the deepest spiritual or esoteric meanings of the Minor Arcana.

The Spear

The bleeding of the Grail Castle is a curious feature of the Grail mythos. Quite early in the development of the story, it was identified with the lance of the Roman centurion Longinus that had pierced the side of Christ during the crucifixion. Along with the Crown of Thorns, this has been regarded throughout the history of Christianity as one of the holiest of relics, next only to the Grail itself. The Lance in the Grail legend is one of the Hallows and appears in the Grail Procession at Carbonek. It is the same lance that wounds the Fisher King, and thus it suggests a link between the Fisher King's wound, if in fact it was dealt by the magical lance, and that of Christ. The bleeding is described either as a continuous stream of blood (as in Wolfram von Eschenbach's *Parzival*) or a single drop (as in Chretien) or as three drops. In the Vulgate *Quest del Saint Graal,* in what is now called the "Lancelot-Grail Cycle," Galahad takes blood from the spear and touches the Fisher King's wound with it, which immediately heals him. The spear corresponds to the element of Fire, the Spear of Lugh, and the suit of Wands.

The Grail

The Grail is variously described as a cup or a deep dish, though Wolfram von Eschenbach links it with the Philosopher's Stone of alchemy. He describes it as a stone which fell from Heaven, but which still retains the associations with food and sustenance we have already encountered in the cauldron of the Dagda and the pantry of Brigid. In the earlier works of the Grail legend, the word *graal* is not explained, but not long after Chretien wrote his poem, the monk Hélinand of Froidmont defined the similar word *gradale* as meaning *scutella lata et aliquantulum profunda,* "a wide and slightly deep dish." Only later, in Robert de Boron's *Joseph of Arimathea,* was the Grail finally identified as the cup or chalice used by Christ at the Last Supper. In the *Perlesvaus,* the Grail can appear in any one of five different forms. The Grail corresponds to the element of Water, the Cauldron of the Dagda, and the suit of Cups.

The Sword

Another magical weapon is the sword that appears in the Grail procession at the mysterious castle of Carbonek and is often depicted as a broken sword. In some versions it seems to have been the sword, rather than the lance, that injured the Fisher King and thus caused the wasting of the land. The task of the Questing Knight—whether Gawain, Perceval, or some other—may be to ask a significant question, or it may be to mend the broken sword. It has been suggested by various commentators that the motif of the broken sword is derived from an Irish myth in the cycle of stories surrounding the legendary Finn MacCool. The hero Cailte and a companion enter an Otherworld castle in which the host was a character called Fergus Fair-hair. Fergus asked Cailte to repair a broken sword that the Tuatha De Danann had refused to mend—this, of course, is the Sword of Nuada which we have already discussed. Cailte did so, and also mended a spear and a javelin. Fergus revealed that each of these weapons was destined to destroy one of the enemies of the gods. After three days, Cailte and two companions left with the weapons. They came to a castle of women, often known in Grail mythology as the Castle of Damsels, where they were attacked by these same enemies of the gods; in the battle, each of the three weapons destroyed one of the enemies. The Sword corresponds to the element of Air, the Sword of Nuada, and the suit of Swords in the Minor Arcana.

The Dish

In Chrétien's account of the Grail procession at Carbonk, there is a *tailléor*, or "carving dish," of silver. In the Didot Perceval, there are two of these dishes. In Wolfram's account in *Parzival*, there are instead two silver knives; it has been suggested that Wolfram had some difficulty in translating the word *tailléor*, although Jessie Weston noted that two knives were to be found as relics at the Abbey of Fescamp in France along with other objects mentioned in the Grail mythos, and thus were related to the Grail in its transformation from Celtic myth to Christian mysticism. The Dish corresponds to the element of Earth, the Stone of Fal, and the suit of Pentacles in the Minor Arcana.

The cards of the Minor Arcana refer to the outcome of events and are more open to specific interpretation than the deeply symbolic cards of the Major Arcana. A preponderance of one suit in a spread would imply that the immediate concerns of the querent are likely to be in that area of their life.

Love

Ace of Cups, Two of Cups, Ten of Cups

The Ace of Cups is the greatest of joys—the blessing of Heaven. It represents not only the fulfilment of attraction between lovers, but something far greater. It is a manifestation of The Holy Grail, for, as we have seen, the four suits not only

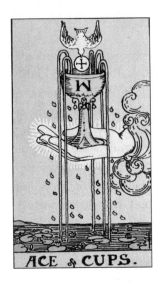

ACE of CUPS.

represent the four elements, but they also represent the four treasures of the Grail: the magical wand, the Grail itself, the sword that pierced Christ's side, and the dish which holds a fish (symbolic of Christ).[38] This Ace demonstrates how love is the greatest power in the universe. Through love comes the discovery that being *selfless* is the key to revealing everything that is beyond earthly life. The soul is set free to roam the heavens in the company of angels.

The Two of Cups represents a union that is marked by spirituality and equality. It is an ideal, but one which is always possible when manifested on the earthly plane. If this card appears when the querent asks about the possibility of love coming into their life, there is reason for joy and celebration.

The requisite patience, understanding, and respect that are tacit in the Two of Cups have their reward later in the Ten of Cups. This is the "happily ever after" card and none the worse for that. The supreme joy that the image evokes is proof against any interpretation of empty sentimentality. The emotional world of the Suit of Cups has reached fulfilment in the material world.

Illusion

Six of Cups, Seven of Cups, Eight of Swords, Nine of Swords

The tarot works on many levels. The student should meditate upon every card in the Rider-Waite deck until every atom of meaning has been distilled from it. To the beginner, the images

---

38   See Strong, Gordon, *The Grail Discovered* (Flash Magic, 2008).

are unfamiliar and often puzzling, but prolonged study will have the effect of unconscious revelation. The "six" card in each suit has a hidden agenda, and the Six of Cups is a particularly telling example. At first glance, it appears to be a touching and affectionate tableau and reunion. The more one looks into it, the odder the scene appears to be. The strange proportion of the figures has the effect of distorting age and youth, accentuated by the equally odd perspective of the buildings around them. All is definitely not rosy in this garden. It is the worst kind of fantasy because it is so empty of genuine feeling—and this is what happens when one revisits memories over and over, especially those from childhood.

Deciding what is real and what is not becomes a continuous theme in the tarot. The Seven of Cups is a graphic description of the kind of quandary we may find ourselves in. None of the choices on offer seem at all appealing, yet many would select one or more of them. These seven cups contain a dragon-like figure, a castle on a steep hill, a golden laurel, a pile of shining jewels, a snake, a maiden's head, and a shrouded figure surrounded by a red light: power, love, riches, revenge. An erroneous belief in what makes for happiness is the cause of so much pain.

Being blind to our lot is another reason for distress, as the Eight of Swords demonstrates. Although they are unable to see, the figure's feet are not bound, so there *is* a way out from their prison, but unfortunately, they are simply not able to see or comprehend it. This card lets us know that at times we are all our own worst enemies.

The Nine of Swords shows the state of anxiety that happens when the conscious mind interprets everything negatively, giving rise to an unending depression. Here, the impression controls the mind, and the unfortunate victim, plagued with worry and insomnia, cannot shake it off.

Gain

Ace of Pentacles, Four of Pentacles, Nine of Pentacles

Achievement in the material world and the effects that state brings to us is one of the themes of the suit of Pentacles. The Ace of Pentacles is a powerful symbol for the munificence of the Earth. All we could possibly need is there for the taking, the only consideration being that we must learn how to work *with* nature.

Wealth is only converted energy, and if we regard it as a moving, flowing force, then it can never be a burden. Problems in the material plane only occur when we hold on too tightly to our possessions. We own nothing of the world; all of it is on loan. Also, we should never desire what we do not need. That way lies ruin. The image of the Four of Pentacles card makes this clear. This figure may look content, but it is only temporary. There is a certain desperation in their look—a fear that once they loosen their grip, they might lose everything. If this happens, they will not have the spiritual reserve to cope with the situation.

The Nine of Pentacles tells a different tale altogether. Here, we see the fruits of effort and dedication resulting in an earthly paradise. The lady in her garden fully deserves all she has achieved and enjoys the pleasures of her kingdom.

Loss

Two of Pentacles, Five of Pentacles, Six of Pentacles

Two represents balance, and in the Two of Pentacles, we contemplate the interplay between the elements of Water and Earth. The lemniscate is woven into the design of the card, reminding us that the Pentacles, though strongly linked with the element of Earth and with material wealth or the lack of it, may also embody spirituality as much as the other three suits. "As above, so below" is the inherent wisdom here. The earth reflects Heaven if we could only see it! This is a card of karma, as are The World and The Wheel of Fortune. On a mundane level, it is "balancing the books." Dickens's Mr. Pickwick warns us that once expenditure exceeds income, unhappiness results. Debts, spiritual or material, are burdensome.

Poverty on all levels is the theme of the Five of Pentacles. Here, the only hope for the unfortunate pair in rags is a realization that the way of higher things, symbolized by the light in the window above them, will offer them the warmth and succour they lack. Faith in what has real value is key here.

Wealth equates with power, and the Six of Pentacles demonstrates how this may sometimes be abused without that necessarily appearing to happen. Dispensing charity may be worthy, but not if the gesture is ostentatious or contrived. Then it is merely cynical.

Society

Three of Pentacles, Three of Cups, Ten of Pentacles

The triangle is the first viable form. Although this dynamic always produces a certain tension, it holds enormous power. The concept of The Holy Trinity and other triads in many other faiths reflects this. In the Three of Pentacles, different but not disparate elements come together in union. They combine their individual talents and skills to achieve an end, a cooperative situation that ensures the smooth working of society. Here, the material, intellectual, and spiritual have come together to form a whole.

On the emotional plane, the theme of *celebration* is depicted in the Three of Cups. The harmony established in the previous Arcanum becomes a fount of joy and delight. One is reminded of the Three Graces of Greek mythology, whose presence always endows us with pleasure.

One would expect the family situation depicted in the Ten of Pentacles to be a source of happiness as well, but none of the figures in the scene seem to actually relate to each other. It is as if all the material gain is in evidence but the love that is such an intrinsic part of the Ten of Cups card is markedly absent here on the physical plane. There is distance, a lack of communion.

Fate

Four of Cups, Five of Cups, Nine of Cup

The suit of cups represents feelings, specifically *true* feelings. What are our dreams? What do we wish for? The theme of the Four of Cups is lost opportunities. The attention of the figure is weary, cynical, and so fixed upon what is in front of them that they have lost sight of their true purpose. The single cup that is being offered to them is more valuable than the other three, yet they ignore it.

In the Five of Cups, the individual depicted experiences regret and even possessing the three *full* cups will not reconcile them for the loss of the other two. This is the person who always considers their glass to be "half-empty" rather than "half-full." When it appears in a reading, this card is often warning us not to fall into that trap.

When they arrive at the stage of the Nine of Cups, their situation appears to be resolved. But is this so? Certainly, they have acquired more, but their attitude is still questionable. A sense of being "too pleased with themselves" clouds the picture. We are not even convinced that they truly value what they own; mere possession seems to be their only motive.

Spirit

Ace of Swords, Two of Swords, Four of Swords, Eight of Cups

The Swords cards, being ruled by the element of Air, represent many different states of mind. These may be triumphant or destructive depending upon their purpose. The sword rep-

ACE of SWORDS.

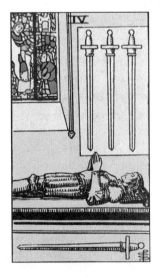

resents the incisive quality of the intellect. The Aces of each suit are the epitome of the element they represent. In the Ace of Swords, we have the triumph that accompanies the winning decision—and acclaim. In the Ace of Swords of the Rider-Waite tarot, the blade is topped by a crown and laurel leaves, flowing down the blade's sides. Victory reflects great glory upon the individual and those who follow them. The sword also represents justice of a worldly nature—a dispute that must be resolved. Not necessarily a physical combat, a war of words could be fought, but the combatants are just as in earnest.

The Two of Swords signifies a decision that has *not* been made and accentuates the fear of making any move. This figure (like the Eight of Swords) is blindfolded. *Not seeing* is often the same as *not wanting to see* in case reality might be too much to bear. But reality always intrudes in the end. This card is the shadow of The High Priestess, who demands that we make a choice, knowing that if we do not, it will be made for us. It is always better to have control of your destiny than to let it slip from your grasp.

The Four of Swords represents a time of rest and reflection. The reclining figure is in deep meditation, their troubles set aside for the moment. Their higher self has taken charge of their being. This is a state of consciousness which we all need to access at one time or another.

In the Eight of Cups, the seeker's quest begins anew as they start upon another phase of their life. They have no qualms about leaving behind what others regard as being essential to life because they have the courage of their convictions as the adventurer—and the light of the Sun and Moon above blesses the enterprise.

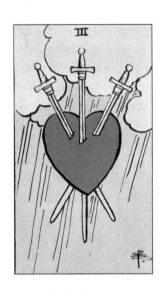

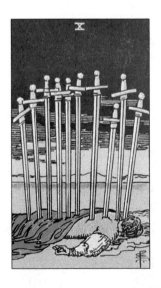

Trial

Three of Swords, Six of Swords, Seven of Swords, Ten of Swords

In the tales of King Arthur, Lancelot must pass over the Bridge of Swords in order to rescue Guinevere. Swords symbolize those thoughts we would rather not admit, and in that sense, they are closely linked with the Jungian concept of the Shadow—all those parts of ourselves which we do not wish to acknowledge. If we do not accept the truth of a situation, then we will fall into the hell of our imaginings. This is why we must not deny our Shadow, but face it with courage, knowing that in time it may become one of our greatest teachers. As the old saying goes, "truth hurts," and swords are sharp. As every magician knows, thought forms are extremely powerful—the starting point of any manifestation. The Temple of the Imagination that the magician creates is as profound as an actual building. We need to come to terms with our responsibility for what we think, for our thoughts create the world. It is as well to remind ourselves that in the universal mind, "idle" or "ugly" thoughts have no place.

The direction in which the swords are pointing is always significant. An upright blade signifies success; one pointing downward, the possibility of ruin. Angled weapons signify conflict. The Three of Swords shows a cloudburst. Although the heart has been wounded, the storm has passed. Any pain that lingers will also eventually disappear.

Regrets feature in the Six of Swords. They linger, a reminder of past woes. The actual swords, which represent these melancholy reminiscences, cannot be taken from the

boat or it will sink. The cloaked, bent figures send the same message of past hurts and sad memories. We must learn to live with our shadow and still continue along the path.

Coping with the ways of the world sometimes means that we indulge in subterfuge. We may get away with it, as the figure in the Seven of Swords seems to be doing, but never should we embrace this kind of morality. When we are the victims of sharp practice, we are not so keen to forgive it.

The Ten of Swords demonstrates the inevitable outcome of mismanagement of our affairs. The card signifies a death, but not a physical one. It is the finality of a phase of life. Surrendering parts of ourselves which are no longer healthy or positive for us is a painful necessity.

Labour

Seven of Pentacles, Eight of Pentacles, Ten of Wands

Effort is energy is reward. Nowhere is this more evident than in the images that mark the suit of Pentacles. Earth energy is the same as any other, although because of its nature, it is often regarded as being static. This is a misconception because all energy is in motion. It is only when we attempt to hold on to a situation that anxiety and pain result.

The Seven of Pentacles depicts a lull which, if it persists, will be damaging—we trust our workman knows this. There is always work to be done, whether it is mental or physical. *Laborare est Orare*—to work is to pray—and we will only be fulfilled if we have an occupation that we love. All employ-

ment may on occasion be tedious or routine, but this can be transformed if one's heart is in the task.

The Eight of Pentacles demonstrates an ideal state. The craftsman proudly displays their work, knowing that those for whom it is intended will recognize its quality. Whatever we produce, even the words we speak, reflects our being. We should mirror a love of the world and make our work a labour of love as well.

We can sometimes make the mistake of taking on too much. The figure in the Ten of Wands is bowed down by their cares. They have too many responsibilities but cannot bear to delegate, believing that only they can captain the ship. A sense of duty is admirable, but a continual struggle is not. The figure in the card literally cannot see the wood for the trees. Inevitably their strength will fail him, and they will fall.

Fulfilment

Two of Wands, Three of Wands

"Travel broadens the mind," which might mean either a physical journey or an expanding of consciousness. In the Two of Wands, a voyage is being contemplated and planned. Maybe the destination has not yet been decided. Perhaps it does not matter where we go, for all paths lead eventually to our destiny. On the journey, we will undergo both elation and disappointment, and these experiences will shape our character.

In the Three of Wands, the traveller waits to embark. They look only ahead, perhaps imagining what they may en-

ACE of WANDS.

IV

VI

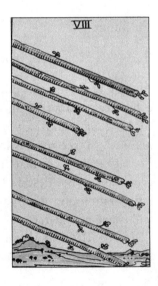

VIII

counter, but always having faith in the outcome. They know that this journey will fulfil them, for this is a time of splendid anticipation, one that will finally reveal their potential.

Courage

Ace of Wands, Four of Wands, Six of Wands, Eight of Wands

Wands are also spears (once flying arrows), so they represent movement or actions about to be carried out. Vitality and potency are associated with this suit—superior energy prevailing in every situation. The Ace of Wands is might, pure and simple. Any enterprise under the influence of this card reaps success in strength and in abundance.

The Four of Wands shows us what can be achieved when enthusiasm is put to a definite purpose. A solid structure that will house beauty and joy is the result. Energy has been positively directed, bringing forth fruitfulness.

The Six of Wands depicts victory, though as in all the sixes, there is something slightly unreal about the scene, something tentative and out of harmony as if it were a play being acted out rather than a real event. Perhaps victory is often hollow, and defeat is simply the other side of a coin which is ultimately worthless. The real value of life's experiences is to show us the next stage of our journey.

The Eight of Wands is an enigmatic image. Are these wands at rest or in motion? Whatever their state, they are in direct contrast to those that are upright or crossed in disharmony. They seem to have a slow and purposeful intent that will eventually be productive.

Conflict

Five of Swords, Five of Wands, Seven of Wands, Nine of Wands

Whenever the number five appears in the tarot, there is discord and conflict. That state is never so marked as the situation in the Five of Swords. The figures are all facing different ways and are concerned only with themselves. One appears to have defeated the others, but the situation is ultimately hopeless. The jagged clouds in the sky tell us that nothing can be resolved until peace returns, hopefully not before too long.

It is the same in the Five of Wands, where the protagonists are all at odds with each other, pulling this way and that as they fight with their wands. This is the barrenness and destruction that results from battle.

In the Seven of Wands, all that can be said is that the one keeps the many at bay. They have gained the upper hand over their adversaries, albeit only temporarily. This is the card of valour—never give up, no matter how heavy the odds are against you.

In the Nine of Wands, combat has simply become a habit. The struggle has no honour; it is merely waste and foolishness. The figure in the card is weary of it all but sees no alternative to the destructive situation in which they find themselves.

CHAPTER FOUR

"The moon may be taken to represent the personality, waxing and waning through innumerable incarnatory phases of reflection of the sun's light or its deflection by the earth's shadow while the Higher Self, the immortal Spirit in man, is rightly symbolized by the sun, which shines perpetually in the heavens, whether we see it or not."

—Dion Fortune, *The Training and Work of the Initiate*

KING of WANDS

QUEEN of WANDS.

KNIGHT of WANDS.

THE COURT CARDS

In a reading, cards of the Major Arcana may or may not represent a person in the querent's life. With the King, Queen, and Knight, the presence of a genuine human individual is always the case. A King represents a mature masculine figure (sometimes a father), a Queen a feminine figure, and a Knight a younger masculine figure. Occasionally, the emphasis may be on the *attitude* of the figure—a King may be "young at heart." The meaning of the Page cards will be discussed separately.

King of Wands, Queen of Wands, Knight of Wands

With Wands, having an affinity with the element of Fire, one would expect active, dynamic, creative characters to emerge in this group. It is the Queen of Wands, affiliated with the sign of Leo, who is the most commanding and authoritative. The King of Wands, although also a regal figure, seems almost placid and disinterested compared to his consort. The Knight of Wands has a boyish innocence about him; he seems the be at the very beginning of his chosen path of knighthood.

KING of SWORDS.

QUEEN of SWORDS.

KNIGHT of SWORDS.

King of Swords, Queen of Swords, Knight of Swords

The depiction of clouds in the suit of Swords cards (the element of Air) denotes the tenor of each card. The King of Swords appears to be above any storms that are brewing, and he is fully in control of his thoughts. The Queen of Swords is associated with the sign of Libra, therefore she also has an affinity with the Major Arcana card of Justice. She seems ready to dispense her judgment with power and purpose in any situation that she encounters. The Knight of Swords, however, is a man of action and not too considerate in his views. A tendency to rashness might be his overriding characteristic; when he appears in a reading, be prepared to encounter someone who acts first and thinks about it later.

KING of CUPS.

QUEEN of CUPS.

KNIGHT of CUPS.

King of Cups, Queen of Cups, Knight of Cups

The King of Cups is an artist, content to dwell in contemplative solitude on an island of his own imagination, surrounded by the sea of his inner vision. He has the power that comes with knowing beauty and the transcendental. The Queen of Cups is an equally assured figure, but with the air of being very secretive. She embodies the characteristics of Scorpio. The Knight of Cups is a dreamy, poetic character, a mystic in quest of the Grail. He has the ways of Pisces and might be sensitive, almost to a fault.

KING of PENTACLES.

QUEEN of PENTACLES

KNIGHT of PENTACLES.

King of Pentacles, Queen of Pentacles, Knight of Pentacles

The bulls' heads that surmount the opulent throne of the King of Pentacles indicate his affinity with the sign of Taurus. He is a man of wealth and earthly power and commands respect because of it. Other aspects of wealth are depicted in various cards in this suit. The Queen of Pentacles has much of The Empress about her, and her love of pleasure and her sensual demeanour are evident. The Knight of Pentacles is the "tall, dark stranger" of many a tale. He is sexually attractive and has an affinity with the sign of Capricorn.

PAGE of PENTACLES.

PAGE of CUPS.

PAGE of SWORDS.

PAGE of WANDS.

Pages

Unlike the King, Queen, and Knight, who always indicate specific individuals in a reading, a Page card more often indicates that a message will come to the querent, the nature of which is determined by the characteristics of the suit. The Page of Pentacles would indicate communications about money or other material issues, the Page of Cups a love letter or a message which is deeply emotionally charged for the querent, the Page of Swords a message warning of potential conflicts in life, and the Page of Wands the announcement of new beginnings, fascinating ventures, and so on. There are times when a Page may represent a person—usually a young and inexperienced individual known to the querent—but in my own experience of readings, this is quite rare.

CHAPTER FIVE

"Truth is within ourselves; it takes no rise
From outward things, whate'er you may believe.
There is an inmost centre in us all,
Where truth abides in fullness."

—Robert Browning, "Paracelsus"

TAROT EXERCISES

The Shingon Buddhist faith recognizes the Smaller and the Greater Universe—whatever occurs in the former is reflected in the latter. Separate but united, each recognizes the nature of the other. In the Western tradition, we usually speak of the microcosm and the macrocosm. The macrocosm encompasses the entire universe, while the microcosm is most often perceived as the human being—not just our bodies, but our consciousness as well.

In the same way, the mystical tarot reflects the earthly plane. Study its images fervently. Observe, do not merely gaze. Notice the shapes of the clouds in the suit of Swords; examine the details of every landscape in the Major Arcana. Time spent in this way will bear fruit. Reflect upon how you respond to particular cards, for your insights are most important. It is the resonance that you set up on the inner planes that is important. Having an ancient, timeless vibration, the tarot holds its forms, thus preventing the initiate from straying into the wilderness of fantasy. The tarot invites a meditative focus.

Meditation is the foundation of magical practice. It is through a sense of existence without being that we gain knowledge greater than that acquired in the "conscious" world. Mastery of the technique of meditation is not gained without constant practice, and many give up after a few attempts. Concentration is essential, and the human mind is notorious for not remaining still, of jabbering and chattering when we wish it to remain focused. Once the key to the practice has been found and the mind is still, however, meditation enables us to contemplate even the most abstruse ideas.

Any meditative work done with individual tarot cards will have a particularly potent vibration. Balance is at the root of understanding the human condition—the way to gain peace for the soul. How does this apply to our studies? As an example, if the student meditates upon the "two" card from each suit of the Minor Arcana, they will gain an understanding of polarity and pairing. How this idea applies to each element will also become apparent, while comparison of the cards with the Grail Hallows may reveal an unexpected spiritual side to situations which initially appeared to be quite worldly. If cards of the tarot are considered together (starting with pairs), they do not assume a hierarchy, but equal parts of a cosmic whole.

While the ways that one may practice meditation on the tarot are as numerous as the grains of sand upon the shore, there are two common, basic approaches to the art. One of them is spontaneous and intuitive, while the other is tightly focused and requires a great deal of concentration.

The intuitive or spontaneous approach is probably the one most commonly practiced—drawing a card at random from the deck and regarding it as your "card of the day." As always, the minutiae of the card are to be examined and contemplated—the clouds in the sky, the landscape that forms the background of the card, as well as the human figures and their facial expressions, their apparent outlook on the situation described by the card, how they are attired, and the things that they hold or carry. But more than study, one poses to oneself the intuitive question: *why did I pull this particular card and how does it affect the conduct of my life today?* If you have pulled the Ten of Cups, consider the blessings you have received in life, and give thanks for them. If your card for the day is the Eight of Swords, ask yourself where in your life you feel trapped (job? Relationship? Lodging?) and what you can do to set yourself free. Of course, it is entirely possible that pulling a card spontaneously from the deck without thinking about it may result in your subconscious choosing the same card two or three times in the course of a couple of weeks. This will clue you in to the fact that the image on the card represents an issue in your life which is important and requires some deep inner work on your part in order to be resolved. And that is valuable information indeed!

Another way to study the tarot is with one's intellect. This is especially useful in the study of the Major Arcana since these are the cards with the symbolic depth of the tarot in all its power and magic. Begin with The Fool and continue with the other cards in their proper order. Place the Arcanum you are studying in a prominent place for meditation—on your altar or your study desk, for example. Spend some time each day in contemplation of the Arcanum. Study each detail of the image, pondering its various possible meanings. Read widely about what different writers have said about the card you are studying. It generally takes a few weeks to master each Arcanum—an intellectual journey through the Major Arcana may take as long as a year, but it will be a year well spent.

And yet, the intellectual journey through the Major Arcana need not be entirely mental. For many years now, a blank deck of the Major Arcana—line drawings of each card without colours—has been available through the Builders of the Adytum. The idea is to get to know each Arcanum by using some type of artistic medium to colour each card yourself. This is a useful supplement to your intellectual journey through each card because it infuses your knowledge of every Arcanum with kinaesthetic, physical knowledge; your studies go beyond the intellect and become implanted in your physical body as well. When you are done illustrating each card in your own extremely personal deck, you can move on to the next Arcanum, studying it with your mind as described above while, at the same time, infusing your physical body with a very deep personal knowledge of the card.

Colour

If you choose to illustrate your own deck, you will soon become immersed in the colours with which Pamela Colman Smith expressed deep spiritual concepts. It is rather unfortunate that modern versions of the Rider pack have not retained the range of tones of the original edition. As would be expected, the colours used in the cards adhere to the traditional qualities assigned to them.

Colour	Attributes
Red	Eagerness and Passion
Orange	Courage and Creativity
Yellow	Harmony

Colour	Attributes
Green	Spirituality and Healing
Blue	The Intellect
Purple	Insight and Compassion
White	Purity of Motive

The power of symbols can never be underestimated. By allowing them to work upon the unconscious mind, great revelations about the tarot will follow. Significant symbols include the rose, water in all its moods, animals and birds, angels, the crown, nakedness, and so on. The inner planes respond to archetypes, and the soul recalls images that are timeless. In the collective unconscious, as Jung calls it, there reside those marker posts that lead us on journeys of cosmic consciousness and reveal to us the full spectrum of the tarot as a universal language.

Numerology

Each number has its own individual character, and the science of numbers is one of the primary foundations of mysticism. Religious buildings were once constructed according to the principles of sacred geometry. This is as apparent in the design of the Pyramids and Chartres Cathedral, among others. We can only marvel at number systems such as *magic squares,* the Fibonacci Series, and the mathematical proportions that relate each planet to its neighbour.[39] The golden ratio, the *vesica piscis,* the pentagram, and the proportions contained in spirals and labyrinths: all these phenomena are magickal and wondrous. Twenty-two, the number of the Major Arcana, is a master number. Eleven is the number of the teacher and doubles to twenty-two. Make of that what you will!

By adding the individual number of two tarot cards, we may create a further level of wisdom. For example, if we take The Emperor and The Hierophant, IV and V respectively, and make a simple sum of their numbers, 4 + 5 = 9, that is IX, The Hermit. It would seem that the martial and religious qualities have integrated to produce the spiritual seeker. We can also apply the same techniques to the Minor Arcana. The Two of Cups depicts the delights of love, while the Three of Cups shows us the joyous mood and festive activity which love bestows upon us. But if we add the numbers, 2 + 3 = the Five of Cups, which warns us that the delights of love may sometimes fade, leaving us with such a feeling of loss that we fail to remember all the joy and happiness we experienced. Many insights can be discovered in this way and lead to much delightful fascination. The more familiar we can become with the various aspects of the cards, the quicker our insights will come.

The *relationship* of numbers is intrinsic to the Western magical tradition. An effect must have a cause greater than itself, and this is demonstrated when numbers are put in

---

39   Named after Leonardo of Pisa, known as Fibonacci, and published in 1202, the sequence is 0, 1, 1, 2, 3, 5, 8, 13, 21, 34, 55, 89, 144, 233, 377, and so on. After two starting values, each number is the sum of the two preceding numbers. From this, the golden ratio, spiral patterns, and prime numbers may be calculated.

combination. Astrology is also based in part upon the interaction of numbers, their harmonies and tensions. Such sacred science enables us to comprehend space and time and how consciousness might be enhanced. The arts, particularly music and painting, constantly employ these principles to aid the artist in creating the delightful and the sublime.

#	Planetary Association	Key Words
1	The Sun	Beginnings, potential, the individual
2	The Moon	Balance, gentleness, imagination, romance
3	Jupiter	Creativity, growth, authority, results
4	Uranus /Sun	Consolidation, structure, building
5	Mercury	Change, conflict, versatility, communication
6	Venus	Stability, love, luxury, artistry, wealth
7	Neptune /Moon	Psychic abilities, spiritual paths, travel, secrecy
8	Saturn	Power, karma, solitude, isolation
9	Mars	Accomplishment, courage, will
10	Pluto	Completion, transformation, renewal

"These are represented by the twelve signs of the Zodiac, the seven planets, and the four elements, and have their correspondence upon the different planes of existence with the different grades of the celestial hierarchy. The knowledge of these is always one of the carefully guarded secrets of the Mysteries, and never revealed outside their portal."

—Dion Fortune, *The Training and Knowledge of the Initiate*

Correspondences

A *correspondence* is an affinity between "natural forms and spiritual causes." Magick employs the harmonic relationships existing between ideas and objects. In ritual, an "atmosphere" is created, powerful enough to influence the outcome of proceedings. Astrological and numerological links with the tarot are fundamental to an understanding of its structure. A system of correspondences with the Kabbalistic Tree of Life is at the heart of the Western Magical Tradition.[40] The complexity of the Kabbalah makes any detailed discussion of its philosophy beyond the scope of this present work.

---

40   As well as being exhaustively debated for over a century! A. E. Waite, the instigator of the Rider-Waite deck, deliberately avoided using the symbolism of the Kabbalah in the designs he presented to Pamela Colman Smith, the artist. Two other members of the Golden Dawn, W. B. Yeats and Arthur Machen, appear to have been involved in the project, but it seems that neither of them were concerned with Hebraic beliefs.

In the following table, the first column lists the twenty -two Major Arcana cards with their corresponding number. Along with the number of the card, its linear reduction is also included, e.g. 15 = 1 + 5 = 6.

The second column, headed "Astrology," gives the sign of the zodiac or planet which is traditionally associated with each card. The third column assigns a card from the Minor Arcana to certain cards in the Major Arcana with the purpose of enhancing their meaning.[41]

The fourth column demonstrates that certain cards may be paired together. Apart from The Magician and The Fool, adding together the card number of all these pairings gives a total of 23 = 5, which is the number of humanity. For example, II (The High Priestess) + XXI (The World) = 23, which reduces to 5. In the same way, VI (The Lovers) + XVII (The Star) also equals 23, which again reduces to 5.

The fifth column suggests traditional groupings of particular cards. The order of the cards has constantly changed over the centuries. Another method gives:

Man: O, I, V, VI, IX, XII XV
Nature: III, X, XIII, XIV, XVI, XIX, XX
Philosophy: II, IV, VII, VIII, XI, XVII, XVIII

A correspondence also exists between the first ten cards of the Major Arcana and the Ace through Ten of Pentacles. The student should give this their consideration. It is also thought that the first part of the Major Arcana (I–XI) re-

---

41   Based on suggestions by Paul Fenton-Smith, *The Tarot Revealed*.

lates to childhood, and the rest to the spiritual aspects of life. Another proposal is that the Ace, Two, and Three refer to man; Four, Five, and Six to woman; Seven, Eight, and Nine to youth; and Ten to child.

Card	Astrology	Minor Arcana	Major Arcana	Cosmos
0. Fool	Uranus		Magician	Humanity
I. Magician	Mercury		Fool	Humanity
II. High Priestess	Moon	Two of Swords	World	God
III. Empress	Venus	Queen of Pentacles	Judgment	God
IV. Emperor	Aries	King of Wands	Sun	God
V. Hierophant	Taurus	King of Pentacles	Moon	God
VI. Lovers	Gemini	Knight of Swords, Two of Cups	Star	Humanity
VII. Chariot	Cancer	King of Cups	Tower	Humanity
VIII. Strength	Leo	Queen of Wands	Devil	God
IX. Hermit	Virgo	Queen of Pentacles	Temper-ance	Humanity
X. Wheel of Fortune	Jupiter		Death	Universe
XI. Justice (2)	Libra	Queen of Swords	Hanged Man	

Card	Astrology	Minor Arcana	Major Arcana	Cosmos
XII. Hanged Man (3)	Pisces	Knight of Cups	Justice	Humanity
XIII. Death (4)	Scorpio	Queen of Cups	Wheel of Fortune	Universe
XIV. Temperance (5)	Sagittarius	Knight of Wands	Hermit	God
XV. Devil (6)	Capricorn	Knight of Pentacles, Eight of Swords	Strength	Humanity
XVI. Tower (7)	Mars			Universe
XVII. Star (8)	Aquarius	King of Swords	Lovers	Universe
XVIII. Moon (9)	Neptune		Hierophant	Universe
XIX. Sun (1)	Sun	Ten of Cups	Emperor	Universe
XX. Judgment (2)	Pluto		Empress	Universe
XXI. World (3)	Saturn		High Priestess	

This table of correspondences is only the beginning. As we shall see, other tables of correspondences can be designed by the assiduous student to "unveil" countless different aspects of myth and magic.

Since the tarot is a universal language, our understanding of all sorts of metaphysical concepts can be enhanced by matching them with their correspondences in the tarot. As you meditate with the card more and more deeply, more and more often, you will be able to design your own tables of correspondences for virtually any topic you please.

The "language" of the tarot is the language of myth, and all the world's mythologies can be expressed in terms of the Major Arcana through such tables of correspondences. The table given above is very basic and may serve as a foundation, but the possibilities for developing other such sets of correspondences is virtually endless. Greek mythology interfaces with the tarot in correspondences are relatively easy to create, simply by matching the traditional planetary and zodiacal correspondences of the tarot with the Greek deities who match with the planets and sign rulers:

Card	Astrology	Greek Mythology
0. Fool	Uranus	Ouranos, Prometheus[42]
I. Magician	Mercury	Hermes
II. High Priestess	Moon	Selene, Artemis
III. Empress	Venus	Aphrodite
IV. Emperor	Aries	Ares
V. Hierophant	Taurus	Aphrodite
VI. Lovers	Gemini	Hermes
VII. Chariot	Cancer	Selene, Artemis

42   The identification of the planet Uranus with the Greek Titan and helper of humankind Prometheus was first suggested by astrologer Richard Nolle in many of his writings.

Card	Astrology	Greek Mythology
VIII. Strength	Leo	Helios, Apollo
IX. Hermit	Virgo	Hermes
X. Wheel of Fortune	Jupiter	Zeus
XI. Justice (2)	Libra	Aphrodite
XII. Hanged Man (3)	Pisces	Poseidon, Zeus, Dionysus[43]
XIII. Death (4)	Scorpio	Hades, Ares
XIV. Temperance (5)	Sagittarius	Zeus
XV. Devil (6)	Capricorn	Kronos (Saturn)
XVI. Tower (7)	Mars	Ares
XVII. Star (8)	Aquarius	Ouranos, Prometheus, Kronos (Saturn)
XVIII. Moon (9)	Neptune	Poseidon, Dionysus
XIX. Sun (1)	Sun	Helios, Apollo
XX. Judgment (2)	Pluto	Hades
XXI. World (3)	Saturn	Kronos

The enthusiastic student will not hesitate to experiment with the mythological systems which lie closest to their own hearts. We shall draw some examples from the legends of King Arthur and his knights, for they are known and loved throughout the English-speaking world. Here is a very simple circle of correspondences which uses the four suits of the Minor Arcana to illuminate the character and relationships of Merlin, the great magician of the Arthurian sagas.

---

43   The identification of the planet Neptune with the archetype of Dionysus was suggested by another astrologer, Liz Greene, in various writings.

MORGANA
North, Earth, And Pentacles

▽
N

▽ W ✦ E △

S

△

NIMUE
West, Water, and Cups

MERLIN
East, Air, and Swords

ARTHUR
South, Fire, and Wands

Here, the placement of Merlin in the east with the element of Air and the suit of Swords accentuates the power of the mind, particularly his own magickal mind. King Arthur's placement in the south, with the element of Fire and the suit of Wands, shows us the creative nature of their association with each other. Opposite Merlin, in the west, is Nimue, the nymph of the lake who stole away Merlin's magick and held him captive with her beauty. In the legends of Merlin, she represents the suit of Cups because his relationship with her is a matter of feeling and emotion. Finally, the sorceress Morgan le Fay, who can become either his friend or his adversary, stands in the north, for their interaction bends and shapes the worldly matters which surround them and are therefore represented by the element of Earth and the suit of Pentacles.

Simple circles like this are only the beginning. The entire mythos of the Arthurian legends can be linked with the tarot, as we see here.[44]

Card	Astrology	Arthurian Mythology
0. Fool	Uranus	
I. Magician	Mercury	Merlin
II. High Priestess	Moon	The Lady of the Lake
III. Empress	Venus	Guinevere
IV. Emperor	Aries	King Arthur
V. Hierophant	Taurus	Guinevere
VI. Lovers	Gemini	Merlin

---

44   See Strong, Gordon, *Sun God, Moon Maiden* (Crossed Crow Books, 2023).

Card	Astrology	Arthurian Mythology
VII. Chariot	Cancer	The Lady of the Lake
VIII. Strength	Leo	King Arthur
IX. Hermit	Virgo	Merlin, Elaine
X. Wheel of Fortune	Jupiter	
XI. Justice (2)	Libra	The Lady of the Lake
XII. Hanged Man (3)	Pisces	The Fisher King, Perceval, Elaine
XIII. Death (4)	Scorpio	Morgan le Fay, Lancelot
XIV. Temperance (5)	Sagittarius	Galahad
XV. Devil (6)	Capricorn	King Arthur, Lancelot
XVI. Tower (7)	Mars	
XVII. Star (8)	Aquarius	Perceval
XVIII. Moon (9)	Neptune	The Fisher King
XIX. Sun (1)	Sun	King Arthur
XX. Judgment (2)	Pluto	
XXI. World (3)	Saturn	

As can be seen, the universality of the tarot is capable of illuminating any path of wisdom, myth, and magic. Even those who devote a lifetime to the study of the cards will never run out of possibilities for a deeper understanding of the magical world that surrounds us all. May your travels along the road of the tarot be powerful, illuminating, and fulfilling.

RECOMMENDED READING

Butler, Bill. *The Definitive Tarot.* Hutchinson, 1975.

Crowley, Aleister. *Magick in Theory and Practice.* 1929.

Fenton-Smith, Paul. *The Tarot Revealed.*
Simon and Schuster, 1995.

Fortune, Dion. *The Mystical Qabalah.* Ibis, 1981.

Ozaniec, Naomi. *The Watkins Tarot Handbook—The
Practical System of Self Discovery.* Watkins, 2005.

Richardson, Alan. *The Magician's Tables—A Complete Book
of Correspondences.* Godsfield Press, 2007.

Sadhu, Mouni. *The Tarot.* George Allen and Unwin, 1962.

Tomberg, Valentin. *Meditations on the Tarot—
A Journey into Christian Hermeticism.* Penguin, 1985.

BIBLIOGRAPHY

Blake, William. *Auguries of Innocence*. 1863.

—. *The Marriage of Heaven and Hell*. Norton, 1975.

Butler, Bill. *The Definitive Tarot*. Hutchinson, 1975.

Crowley, Aleister. *Magick in Theory and Practice,* 1929.

Dickens, Charles. *The Pickwick Papers*, 1905.

Fenton-Smith, Paul. *Tarot Revealed*. Allen and Unwin, 2008.

Fortune, Dion. *The Mystical Qabalah*. Ibis, 1981.

Michell, John F. *Confessions of a Radical Traditionalist*. Dominion, 2005.

Ozaniec, Naomi. *The Watkins Tarot Handbook—The Practical System of Self Discovery*. Watkins, 2005.

Richardson, Alan. *The Magician's Tables—A Complete Book of Correspondences*. Godsfield Press, 2007.

Sadhu, Mouni. *The Tarot—A Contemporary Course of the Quintessence of Hermetic Occultism*. George Allen and Unwin, 1964.

Strong, Gordon. *Question of Magick*. Flash Magic Press, 2007.

—. *The Grail Discovered*. Flash Magic Press, 2008.

—. *Sun God, Moon Maiden*. Crossed Crow Books, 2023.

—. *Merlin: Master of Magic*. Crossed Crow Books, 2023.

Tomberg, Valentin. *Meditations on the Tarot—A Journey into Christian Hermeticism*. Penguin, 1985.

Tompkins, Sue. *Aspects in Astrology*. Random House, 2001.

Wang, Robert. *The Qabalistic Tarot: A Textbook of Mystical Philosophy*. Marcus Aurelius Press, 2004.

Wordsworth, William. *Intimations of Immortality*. 1895.